Secrets

of Dating and Mating
After Medicare

A Journey Into the Incredible World of
Dating, Loving, and Marrying
of Singles Over 60

ELEANOR VALE

ADVANCE PRAISE FOR

Secrets of Dating and Mating After Medicare

"Stories are effective vehicles to inform, educate and inspire. The stories in SECRETS of DATING and MATING after MEDICARE were an easy and enjoyable read. Ms. Vale captured the essence of the perceived problems from the mouth of the seniors themselves. The chapter on Mortality and Other Discomforts shows clearly that she did her homework, as the anti-aging process, both physically and mentally is now our central mission as a generation. Supplements, Hormones, diet and lifestyle have all taken on a new meaning. A well-worth read!"

– Marcia A. Harris MD – Wellness and Preventative Medicine DrMarciaHarris.com – The Life Balance Center of New York

"Eleanor Vale's Secrets is tantalizing, fascinating, illuminating and instructive. She is a modern-day Studs Terkel for a world neglected in the media, namely Romance and Dating for Seniors."

– JIM JERMANOK, Award Winning Filmmaker, Speaker and Author of *BEYOND THE CRAFT: What You Need To Know To Make A Living Creatively!*

"A concise, enlightening, and entertaining book of the choices facing the Over the Rainbow crowd. Vale's journey and her interviewees show us there really are bluebirds flying over the rainbow. A must read for everyone over 60. And for their children, too."

– Helane Royce, CEO

HerRoyalHanger, Newport Beach, CA

"Timing is everything... especially in Life and in Dating. Vale's ability to tell the story of how she and many other seniors were able to get back into the "Dating World", making a quantum leap from the side lines into dating again will give many seniors the inspiration and guidance to come out and join their contemporaries in the Fun World of dating again."

– Warren Weideman

Film and TV Producer, New York

"Sexy at 60, 70, 80, 90? You bet! Vale takes us on a rollicking ride through the brave new world of senior dating, mating and marrying, and shows us how it just may be better the second, third, fourth time around. Later life romance has its special trials, but Vale shows us it's well worth the effort."

– Madelyn Jaye, Divorce Attorney

New York

Publisher:

Re-Set My Clock, LLC

Publisher's Address:

141 East 56th Street - Suite 3H

New York, New York 10022

ISBN:

Softcover: 978-1-7331827-0-6

Hardcover: 978-1-7331827-1-3

Ebook: 978-1-7331827-2-0

All names of interviewees have been changed for privacy.

Illustrations by ANTONIA AVIVA CAFFREY
Instagram: Avivashiryan

Websites:

https://ResetMyClock.com
https://Secretsofdatingandmatingaftermedicare.com
https://Happydaysafter60.com

https://Instagram.com

@eleanorvale
@secretsofdatingandmat
@happydaysafter60

https://Facebook.com

Eleanor Vale
Secrets of Dating and Mating After Medicare
Re-set My Clock @resetmyclock1
Happy Days After 60

Email:

Eleanor.Vale@resetmyclock.com

TABLE OF CONTENTS

To all the seniors out there

who consented to be interviewed.

And to life itself.

FOREWORD

THIS IS A CONTEMPORARY, MULTI-VOICED STORY of men and women who have been in the singles world of dating, loving, and forming relationships in their sixties, seventies, eighties, and nineties.

This book has grown out of my personal experience.

This book is based upon interviews with about 100 real seniors.

I became a widow at seventy-four years old. My husband and I were married for forty-four years. Much to my surprise, men who were known to both my husband and me called me. Initially, perhaps shyly, they would say something like, "Sorry about Peter, would like to get together with you and reminisce about old times." Then some friends, male and female, called and said, "We know someone who is a widower...divorced, whom you might like. May I give him your name?"

It dawned on me at the ripe age of seventy-four that although my marriage may be over, my life was not over. I even began to quip, "There is life after death, provided the death is not your own."

This book originally was entitled *Dating and Mating After Menopause*. That would mean it was aimed at the fifty-somethings and up. But as I began my journey of new self-awareness as to my emotional needs, and as I looked at the world around me, I realized that the sixty-somethings plus (and well into the nineties, as you shall see), consisted of a somewhat *different population* from the "menopausers."

And that we have a very small collective voice, and our adventures, our needs, and our opinions need a chronicle of our own.

Hence the title: *Secrets of Dating and Mating After Medicare*.

A few comments on what you are going to read about.

You are going to read there is a new definition of "old" out there. It used to be sixty-five. Right? Time of retirement, many folks (mostly men) did not even make it to sixty-five. No longer. And you will see why.

You are not going to see much reference to the word "old" in this book. Maybe none. Being old is a shifting landscape. You will read why as you read the chapters "Sex and the Single Senior" and "Busy, Busy, Busy," and the chapter written by "King Arthur," my male guest writer.

This book is not trying to deny reality. On the contrary. Through the many voices of my interviewees, you will understand the new reality for seniors. So please suspend judgment until you finish.

I interviewed more than 100 folks, male and female, in their sixties, seventies, eighties, and nineties, for their *singles* experiences. You will see evidence of how and why we feel better despite our growing infirmities.

My first chapter is titled "Parachuting Back In." That is how my journey began. Come join me.

CHAPTER ONE

PARACHUTING BACK IN

I SCANNED THE RESTAURANT QUICKLY, LOOKING FOR a man sitting alone.

My girlfriend Nancy had asked me whether I was ready to start dating again. There was someone she wanted me to meet. It was around four months after Peter had passed away. I heard myself say I was ready. A few minutes after Nancy's call, David called, introduced himself as Nancy's friend, and invited me to dinner at the New York Athletic Club. The NYAC is a club where Peter and I belonged for over forty years and where I felt totally comfortable. I said yes. I described myself as blonde-haired. The call lasted less than two minutes.

My heart started pounding. I picked up the phone. I called my older (forty-three-year-old) son. He picked up immediately. I said, "Hi, my girlfriend wants to fix me up with a blind date. What do you think?" (I was lying, as I already had said yes.) His response was immediate, and one which I will never forget: "Sure, Mom, why not?"

Heart still pounding, I made a second call—to my younger (forty-year-old) son. He also picked up immediately. I said the exact same thing to him, "Hi, my girlfriend wants to fix me up with a blind date. What do you think?" His response was simply one word, uttered strong and clear: "GREAT."

I am widowed at seventy-four years old. This was to be my first date after forty-four years of marriage. I could see I was experiencing the same feelings that I'd felt many years earlier—even a lifetime ago. I was anxious, fearful, expectant, needing to feel good about myself. I didn't dare use the word "sexy."

How should I dress? I need to be attractive enough, flirtatious, alluring, but not inappropriate for someone my age. Do single women dress differently from married women? Do single women in their seventies dress differently from single women in their thirties? What is "dress appropriate?" How sexy should I look in my seventies? How sexy *can* I look in my seventies? What does a widowed grandmother in her seventies wear on her first date?

I tried on at least half of all my clothes. I must have emptied my entire closet. My bed was piled high with slacks, blouses, skirts, dresses, bags, and shoes. My bedroom looked like a war zone. With each try-on, I looked in the mirror, and asked myself, "Is this right for now?" I was not really able to answer the question with any assurance.

***

Now, nervously, I enter the NYAC restaurant. My heart is pounding once again. The maître d' escorts me toward the windowed tables. I look for my date. There are a few men sitting alone. Suddenly, an old-looking man smiles and waves in my direction. He is wrinkle-skinned and bald. This old man could not have been waving at me! I turn my head to look behind me, wondering who this old man was waving at. But there is no one behind me! Then I realize, with a pop, he means me! What happened? How could I be dating this old man?

***

The shock of self-recognition! The shock of reality!

I am living in a different time, but feeling as I did many, many years ago. I have the same anxiety, the same feelings I had as a young woman when I started dating. Here I am in my seventies with the same expectations I had as a teenager. I expected to see a much younger-looking man.

Now, forty-four years later, I am much older, with children and grandchildren. I know that. My face is wrinkled. My body has changed. Yes, I also know my husband lost his hair. But I simply forgot. It had been slow and gentle. I had lived with my aging. I had lived with my husband's aging. And now, in the face of this smiling old man, I was facing myself.

My blind date clearly identified me as age appropriate. But I failed to identify him.

Am I simply an old woman dating an old man? And what does that mean?

We "seniors" have been married a long time, or have had a long-time serious relationship, or maybe have been away a long time somewhere on a desert island. The point is we have been "out of circulation" for a long enough time to feel that we are parachuting into a dating world different, but similar, to an earlier time in our lives.

It feels the same. But it looks different. Will it feel different going forward?

And this is why I've titled my first chapter, "Parachuting Back In."

SOME SHOCKS OF RE-ENTRY

1 — Dinner at 5:00 P.M.

When did it happen that dinner is at 5:00 or 6:00 p.m., not at 8:00 or 9:00 p.m.?

Here it was only 6:00 p.m. and I was eating dinner. Which means, given the usual one to two hours for dinner, I could easily be home by 9:00 p.m.

2 — New Meaning for P.T.

When did it happen that we stopped working out with our Personal Trainer and now work with our Physical Therapist? When did it happen that "going to the gym" was more for rehabilitation than for getting buff?

The last time I took notice, we went to the gym and some of us paid extra for personal trainers. Now for the older folk, PT means physical therapist, and paid for by our insurance company.

I sit here in the restaurant at 6:00 p.m. My blind date tells me about his session with his physical therapist. Thanks to PT, his sciatica is under control; his fractured toe is improving.

I remind myself when Peter would meet me for dinner at the NYAC at 7:30 p.m. He would have just come from his workout with his personal trainer. He would flex his newly exercised muscles and smile.

3 — The New Dressing Up Is the Old Dressing Down

It was probably happening when I was in my fifties, but I didn't notice. Peter and I as a married couple simply continued to do what we had been doing for years. When did people stop dressing up for Friday night dates, and instead dress down on Fridays? When did men remove their jackets? Their ties? Their collared shirts for their first dates? Not the last time I looked.

In my old days of dating, I wore my casual, conservative outfits during the week. For our nights out with my husband, I dressed up! You know, heels, jewelry.

Things that made me feel good about myself and, in turn, made me feel feminine and alluring.

4 — When Did Women Begin to Ask for Men's Business Cards?

I don't go back so far that I always had to wait for the "phone to ring." But I was not prepared for the forward, aggressive posture women use today in the dating world. Women, as often as not, are making the first move. This was a new world that I had to learn to navigate. I covered this topic in a chapter of its own, "Single Seniors Are Very Busy."

5 — When Did Women Start Paying for Men?

The last time I looked, a guy called me up and asked for a date. And if I said yes, he came over, picked me up, took me wherever, all on his dime. This was the courtship game. Even it was a blind date.

This method of courtship had changed drastically, which I was to find out. But more about this, in a chapter of its own, which I titled, "Money, Money, Money."

6 — How Come All My Dates Have Almost No Hair?

The last time I dated, all the men had hair. And lots of it. Sure, I noticed that men were losing their hair. Even Peter had lost a lot of his hair. But I never dated a balding or bald-headed man before. It just didn't feel right. Something was out of kilter.

I realized I was on a new adventure—an adventure that no one had prepared me for.

This book is about re-entering the singles' world, and not being able to pick up where we left off. We are not able to replicate entirely the old social world we knew.

We bring to our new single life the same fears and anxieties, the same attitudes we experienced as much as twenty, thirty, forty, even fifty years ago.

But we soon learn we need to navigate the new landscape. And we bring a different mix of fears, anxieties, and attitudes.

That is why I wrote this book, and that's why I titled it *Secrets of Dating and Mating After Medicare.*

This book is your journey into the future...as you remember the past. You will read interviews and conversations from some of the more than 100 men and women I interviewed, who are going through what you're going through. The same fears, the same anxieties, that you may be experiencing now, for the same reasons you are experiencing them. Also, the same exhilaration of the chase, the infatuation, the chemistry of meeting someone, and the bonding in a relationship of your choice.

LET THE JOURNEY BEGIN.

HE WANTS to MEET ME IN PERSON BUT I'M NOT READY FOR THAT LEVEL OF INTIMACY.

CHAPTER TWO

DATING – BUSY, BUSY, BUSY:

No Retirement for the Senior Single

BACK THEN. IT IS 1986. MY SEVENTY-SIX-YEAR-OLD mother-in-law Pearl, sitting in her high-backed living room chair, had just announced she intended to start dating. I could have fallen off my chair. What was this old woman thinking? Was she off her rocker? She was seventy-six years old!

Her husband, my father-in-law, also seventy-six years old, had just passed away. Pearl was a lively, fun-loving, charismatic woman—despite her complaints of arthritis, her hearing loss, and her vision loss. Her spirit was bubbly. One of her favorite expressions was, "I am a young person trapped in an old body." So I knew she was serious and made no attempt to dissuade her (as if I could).

True to her word, Pearl went out into the world, alone, foraging for a guy. Promptly, she joined the English-Speaking Union, a Theater Club, and even took a few golf lessons.

After a few months, once again seated in her high-backed chair, Pearl announced that she was calling it quits. All the men she met were either younger and tried to sell her financial or accounting advice, or it was some guy who was looking to be squired around Manhattan café society hot spots with an old rich lady. For her to have met an eligible man, Pearl said, she would have had to read the obituaries, show up at the widow's gravesite, and tackle the new widower in order to beat out the overwhelming number of widows out there.

Until the day she died, at the age of eighty-eight, some twelve years later, she complained that her older years were so lonely.

In 1986, older women outnumbered older men by about two to one.

Fast forward to today. Pearl today, yes, at seventy-six years old, would have had options she would never have dreamed of in 1986.

*A*ND NOW. GLORIA JUST RETURNED FROM A rehabilitation center. At seventy-six years old, she fell down the stairs of her two-story family home, the one she'd obtained in her hard-fought divorce from her husband of thirty-five years. She broke her hip and the doctors put her back together again with a bunch of plates, screws, and rods. I enter the living room. I find her sitting in a high-backed chair next to the window, her walker by her side. On seeing me, she carefully puts aside the item she had been working on. If the year had been in my mother-in-law's era, it probably would have been a crossword puzzle, a book, maybe knitting or something like that. But now, it was an iPad tablet.

"So what were you doing on the iPad?" I asked. Gloria answered, "Sending a couple of flirts." Surprised, I commented, "Honey, you can't even walk right now. Why bother with a dating website?" Gloria smiled and glowered at me at the same time. "I may not want to meet anyone new on a walker. That feels a bit much for a first date. But I expect to be on a cane in a few weeks..." Her voice trailed off. Then she started again.

"Eleanor, you have no idea how many men I meet for the first time who come in with hearing aids. And we spend the coffee, or drink hour, with my having to raise my voice and repeat myself. They may be on a cane. Or if they have no physical aids, I can see they have trouble walking."

"Well, do you see them again? Isn't that a turn-off?" I asked.

"Why no," responded Gloria. "I think to myself, 'There but for the grace of God go I. Illness is a reality of dating in our sixties, seventies, eighties, and nineties. I have learned that illness or physical imperfection is not the defining trait for a relationship. It is now simply one more thing to consider in my interest in the person across the table."

WHY IS DATING POSSIBLE NOW

Why is Gloria, in her seventies, able to date now, when my mother-in-law, also in her seventies, was unable to then?

The short answer is because there are more men living longer. The long answer is men are living longer and the Internet makes meeting someone much easier.

A MORE LEVEL PLAYING FIELD

There are more men living into their seventies, eighties, and nineties than ever. Statistics show that there is a much greater pool of senior men out there.

The fact is that between 1989 and 2009, life expectancy for U.S. males grew by 4.6 years, while predicted lifespans for American women rose by 2.7 years, according to the recent report from Institute for Health Metrics and Evaluation. That manly surge has narrowed the life-expectancy gender gap to five years, one month, and six days—compared to a seven-year gulf in 1989. This life-expectancy gap has narrowed even more since 2009.

"Men are catching up," said Dr. Ali Mokdad, professor of global health at the IHME, part of the University of Washington.

According to the Social Security Administration, a man reaching the age of sixty-five in 2013 can expect to live on average until the age of eighty-three. A woman reaching sixty-five today in 2013 can expect to live on average until the age of eighty-five.

Think about that. If you have started receiving Medicare benefits, you can look forward to another twenty years of life! All right, only eighteen if you are a man.

We have pushed Social Security benefits in this country to sixty-seven years old. While economics may have been the motivating force for the government to save money, no one has complained. Indeed, sixty-seven sounds awfully young to most of us nowadays.

If statistics bore you, simply read the obituaries. So many more men die at older ages. So and so was in his high eighties. So and so was in his nineties. David D. Rockefeller died recently at 101. The oldest living person today is a 112-year-old Japanese man. Previously, the oldest living person was a 113-year-old Spanish man. Note the word, "man."

You wonder what shape these folks are in? Well, yes, we are generally in less than 100% health. We are facing arthritis, bad knees, bad backs, that most dreaded of male problems—prostate cancer—and breast cancer, the most dreaded of female problems, plus all the maladies of growing old. Remember what Pearl said at seventy-six, "I am a young person trapped in an old person's body." In Pearl's day, it probably would have stopped us. But today, like Gloria, we are dating anyway. *See chapter on "Mortality and Other Discomforts."*

THE INTERNET

Thank you, Martha Stewart. At seventy-one years old, the fabulous, divine Martha Stewart was reported in the New York Post, April 30, 2013, to have posted her profile on the Internet. Why? As the Post reported it, she said, "'I'd like to have breakfast with somebody. I'd like to go to bed with somebody,' the usually prim and proper seventy-one-year-old media mogul cooed to a stunned Matt Lauer on the [Today] show."

Why would someone like Martha Stewart need or want to meet through a dating website on the Internet? She is a celebrity. Known to everyone. Why would she not be able to meet someone through her normal channels?

Well, folks, that's exactly why Martha joined an Internet dating service. She did not want to meet a man through her "business" connections. In her business connections, she is rational, logical, tough...shows no tears.

She wanted to meet a stranger, who learned about Martha when he took her to a movie and saw her tear up at a very sad scene, or watched her pull out her handkerchief when Madame Butterfly plunged a knife into her stomach as Pinkerton approached with his wife.

Martha Stewart's social problem could be the same as many of ours. Many of us have worked outside the home for many years. A number of us have become quite successful. Older women are leaders in our fields. We earn "good-to-big" money. But we have gotten the reputation that that means we are bossy and control freaks. Too many men whom I've interviewed say that. They assume that Martha Stewart must be a killer socially, a lousy companion, "controlling where I will eat, what I will eat" and "most probably lousy in bed." Why? Because she runs a large organization successfully, so it must be in her acquired DNA (which many men seem to think is possible).

MEETING WEBSITES FOR SENIORS
ARE A BILLION-DOLLAR BUSINESS FOR A REASON

Meeting on a website for seniors is a billion-dollar business for several reasons:

The first, and probably most important, is that there are more of us of both genders, allowing a greater ease of connection. You meet more folks for the time you put into the matter.

It is also a more level playing field to show our personality rather than accomplishments and fragilities. Martha Stewart seems so much more approachable when you see she, too, needs the dating site.

So today, Pearl, at seventy-six, would not have had to leave her high-backed chair to forage for a dating partner. Her grandchild would have put her on the Internet, helped her write a profile, taken some pictures of her...or used pictures of her when she was fifty-five. She could have sat back and at least flirted with the opposite sex to her heart's content. And started having some fun by dating.

Today, unlike Pearl of twenty-five years ago, we can meet and date each other unabashedly, without losing any energy or time. And we maintain our dignity, style, and self-respect at the same time. What could be better?

WHAT IT IS LIKE TO DATE AFTER MEDICARE—
POST SIXTY-FIVE YEARS OLD

— Dan – 71 – Divorced After 44 Years of Marriage —

I ask the question, "What was it like to re-enter the world of dating as a senior?" In response, Dan tells me about his first party. "I felt like a piece of meat. Spent that night in a corner drinking." But then he adds, "Surprisingly, women were coming over to me anyway."

Dan is divorced from his college sweetheart after forty-four years. He just turned seventy-one. A handsome man, over six feet, overweight, but still skis, gardens, and keeps himself as active as his body allows. (But he, too, has a physical therapist, not a personal trainer, to help him overcome his pains.) (*See Chapter 1 – "Parachuting Back In."*)

He continues, "It was strange doing the same things I had done as a teenager. But what was stranger is that I felt the exact same way. Despite the fact I raised two kids, built up a successful business, live in a beautiful house, have standing in the community, I felt nervous, anxious, and exposed."

In answer to my follow-up question, "So why didn't you give up?" he said, "I was lonely for female companionship," and then he smiled and said, "I wanted to get laid."

Did he meet anyone at that party? No, but he went on to say he met new women through a variety of avenues. He joined a sailing club. He joined a ski club. He was introduced to available women through friends. And he uploaded his profile to a senior dating site on the Internet. Which is where I met him.

— Lois – 80 – Widow Twice Over —

Lois declared that for a few years after her widowhood she wasn't interested at all in meeting new men. No, she insists, it wasn't fear or anxiety. "It's just that I was so happy with my husband and had so many financial issues to handle after his death, I just never wanted or needed to expend the energy to meet someone." But Lois admits the day finally came. One day, she woke up feeling lonely, feeling she wanted to feel needed…at whatever level she could get. Lois admits to having "a little anxiety," but then states in the next breath, "Anxiety is natural, so I just sucked my stomach in and went to places where I could expose myself." "And where was that?" I asked. Lois said, "Well, I am not much of a churchgoer, so I went to my college clubs, joined an arts club, and, well…just started moving around."

Lois comes across cool and collected. Meeting a man is a project she has undertaken. She is moving around, meeting people. Hoping to connect. Wanting to connect. Planning on connecting. Keeping her appearance together, putting her best foot forward, and "hoping for the best."

Lois has not used the Internet to enlarge her social world. She believes she doesn't need it, at this point. She believes everyone on the Internet lies. "You have no idea who the person really is."

— George – 74 – Divorced a Long, Long Time Ago —

George wears a toupee. He hates the idea of meeting a woman, as he described it, looking "old and bald." "I keep myself very well groomed, because I know you ladies like it. When I was younger I wouldn't have dared to go out on a first date in a T-shirt or something like that. I had to wear a shirt, tie, and jacket. So when I started going to meet-ups, I did not give it a thought."

George is a retired lawyer. He practiced divorce law for around thirty-five years. At sixty-seven years old, he was delighted he could get out of that game and retire with a satisfactory income to continue living in New York.

He was married once, a long, long time ago. He had two long-time relationships (more than five years), but eventually broke up. "Why?" I asked.

"Both of these women had children who were part of the household. The women were raising them. I had to go along with their lifestyles and obligations. Although initially I accepted the situation, after a while it began to wear on me. Since I never had a family of my own, guess I am just not a family man."

"And now that you are over seventy, how do you feel?" I asked.

George answered he was delighted, because he felt free. The women who he is meeting now are past the child-rearing stage. They are in their sixties and seventies. If they had children, the children are, by and large, grown and gone.

George then reminded me of an old joke. "When does life begin?"

"Life begins when the children get married, and the dog dies."

We both laughed.

George said he never went on a dating site. It was too much trouble. He has used the Internet for meet-ups. There are events in many locations all over the country which bring like-minded people together. Some of them are meant for people over sixty. Some of them are for people over fifty. Some of them do not mention age. There are new types of meeting folks all the time.

He described travel clubs for seniors, cooking classes for seniors, veggie restaurant meet-ups for seniors, bowling for seniors.

When I asked him about his feelings when he went to his first meet-up after a long hiatus from the dating scene, he described his attendance at a ballroom dancing meet-up. "There were women, some with gray hair, obviously over fifty, mostly huddled in a corner talking to each other. There were men, bald-headed men, men with gray hair, and men with hair like mine huddled and standing in another corner talking to each other. It reminded me of my teenage high school parties. It might have been fifty years later, but we don't change. If we were wallflowers as teenagers, we do the same thing in a social situation now. And then there were the brave guys or girls who actually walked across the room to ask the other sex to dance...and as it was with the older folk."

"So what category were you in?" I asked. George said, "I was a huddler. I still am a huddler. So I met no one. I danced with no one. I learned my lesson. I went on a kayak trip for seniors. I didn't meet anyone I wanted to date, but at least I interacted, and came back feeling good about myself."

These are only three of the many stories I heard. The commonality of these stories is that these people have to move out of their comfort zone in order to meet people, but in today's world, there are plenty of places where we can meet.

— Diane - 76 – Widow —

I re-entered the dating world at seventy-four, after fifty years of marriage to one man. I was warned that I would have to kiss many a frog to meet my prince. But I also received that warning when I was last in the dating scene, many, many years ago.

I've never been a slouch about trying new things, so I considered my dating once again a challenge—a fun challenge at that. I met men through friends and through activities that I started going to. I joined a YMCA and went to exercise class. I also started attending book clubs. I've always liked to read. But this time I made sure the meetings I went to included single folk. I stayed away from painting classes, not because I wouldn't like to learn to paint, but because painting classes are generally filled with women.

But to be honest, even if the class was heavily filled with women, I was generally okay with that. I see women as sisters and we can help each other. It wouldn't be the first time where a decent guy and I just did not hit it off, and I passed him along to another single woman.

I am a real estate broker. So I still work. I have to pick and choose my commitments. But I consider finding a new guy a full-time job. So I put lots of effort into it.

I think of myself as pretty self-confident. I don't let setbacks set me back. Rejection, at any age, is not fun. Dating, at any age, in my opinion, is like horseback riding—which I did in my younger years. I fell off a horse once in a while. I was thrown from a horse once in a while. Just like my dating experiences. In the dating situation, I do what I did when I rode horses. I get up, dust myself off, treat my bruises, and get right back up into that saddle again.

The Internet is always there for me. I use it as needed. Without shame. Without expectations. But always with a sense of the challenge.

There were some adjustments for sure. One, which I would like to pass along to your readers. I am rather vain. My husband and I were considered a "beautiful couple." Everyone said that we just looked so good together.

I met a lovely man...who actually was introduced to me by mutual friends. He was a widower. He was on the slim side for a man of almost eighty, and did not have that ugly male paunch. But he was bald. I was not used to bald men. I had never even touched a bald man's scalp. So that took *some getting used to. But he had a bad hook nose. And that really bothered me. It was a turn-off. A serious turn-off.*

I remember talking on the phone to one of my very good girlfriends, Alex. Alex's husband was still alive at the time. So she was not in the singles world at all. She and her husband knew my husband and me over the many years of our marriage. In fact, she may have been the one who coined the initialism "B.C." as shorthand for "beautiful couple" to describe my husband and me. I blurted out that I was dating this lovely man, but his hook nose really turned me off.

Her response was quick: "Oh, forget it, Diane. You are not going to bear his children. Forget about it."

That was an epiphany. It was like a light went on. Alex was absolutely right. What may have been important to me forty years ago is unimportant now. That's when I realized that even though I was back in a dating world again, it was unnecessary, even undesirable, to try to replicate my earlier needs and requirements. So I got past his big hook nose. I found him attractive. And we are still together, five years later.

— **Murray– 71 – Widower** —

Murray was around seventy-one when I met him via one of the dating sites for seniors. I appreciated his self-profile. He claimed to have been an engineer with IBM, was widowed, had three grown children who lived in various parts of the country. We "flirted" a bit on the dating site, and at one point talked on the phone. The problem for me was that he lived in Poughkeepsie, and I lived in New York City. After a while, we both decided we were G.U.—an initialism from my teenage days meaning, "geographically undesirable."

When I decided to write this book about one year after our Internet meeting, I called him up, asked him if he remembered me (to which he answered, "Of course") and asked if I could interview him for the book.

The Internet has been a life-saver for meeting someone. There aren't too many eligible women for me to meet in the Poughkeepsie area, as you can imagine. Yes, there is a lot of baloney on the Internet. Why is it that all you gals like to go for a "walk on the beach?"

To which I retorted, "Why are all you guys six feet?" We both laughed.

It was an investment for me. A small one at that. There were a number of false alarms. Yes, I did meet a woman who was using an alias, and looking to trade her husband in for a new one. But, by and large, it expanded my world, and allowed me to meet someone with whom I was compatible. I like to think I am a more acceptable person.

In my opinion, if you stick with it, you will meet someone. It took me a solid year. But it was less time-consuming, and certainly less expensive, than lots and lots of blind dates.

— David – 67 – Twice Married —

I met David on the Internet. After my guy broke up with me because his kids didn't want him to re-marry, I dusted myself off and put my profile on one of the senior dating sites. David was one who flirted with me. It did not work out, but he was happy to be interviewed for this book.

David was married twice. The first marriage lasted ten years, after which they divorced. He had a son by that marriage. His son was now married with children of his own. He then married a woman named Sheila, whom David described as his real love of his life. She died of cancer after fifteen years of marriage. David said he was heartbroken.

David is a chiropractor, and has a secretary/office manager running his small office. She suggested that he join a single senior site. With his input, she wrote his profile. She took his picture. She uploaded all the information to the website. Every morning, like clockwork (so said David), she not only opened the mail, etc., but examined postings of women. When she thought a woman would be a match for David, she alerted him to the posting.

David never once went on the site himself. When he did agree that the woman looked attractive, he told his secretary to go ahead and flirt. At some point he took over, and spoke to the woman on the phone.

And that's how he met me. I was hand-picked by his secretary/office manager.

— Arnold – 73 – Never Married —

I found Arnold to be downright homely in person. My first contact with him had been through the Internet. He picked up my profile and sent me an email. I looked at his photo and profile and thought he was worth a meet-up at some point. When I met him at a restaurant for the first time, he was unrecognizable from his photograph. Maybe it was that he was wearing horn-rimmed, highly magnified eyeglasses. They seemed to take over his face. Also, he was wearing a beard, something that he did not have in the online photograph.

Arnold, it turned out, had been on that senior website for four years—four years with the same photo. My heart sank as I quickly realized that this was a one-day "date." I shifted quickly to the fact that I was writing this book, and asked if I could interview him. He seemed happy at the thought of being able to express himself candidly about his dating experiences.

Arnold is a working architect, even though he was seventy-six years old at the time of the interview. He stated, with a smile, that he would work until the day he died, or until the time he couldn't remember his own name anymore.

Like a number of older men who have assistants, Arnold said his assistant works the computer. When it comes to dating sites, however, Arnold learned how to navigate them pretty well. He has been on as many as three websites at one time.

He stated that he believed at least 40-50% of women misrepresent themselves. I felt like exclaiming, "like you" but I bit my tongue, so to speak. He continued, "They say they are in good shape. Like Sophia Loren. *Bullshit.*"

He is drawn to women who "take care of themselves" and are between the heights of 5'3" and 5'7". His real attraction comes only during a conversation with a woman. He needs to have an intellectual conversation. He needs to feel he is talking to an intelligent woman. He does not care about her age. But he tends to feel more comfortable with women in his own age group. He likes a woman who is psychologically aware. He was psychoanalyzed for many years and can relate better to women who have been down that road as well.

So when he is checking out the dating websites, he gives a cursory look to her face. He reads carefully whether she has any advanced degrees, whether she is a professional. He tries to get a "read" of her as a person before he even acknowledges her on the Internet. Once he has made contact with a woman, he shifts as quickly as possible to a phone call. There may be several phone calls between the two, before anything like a meet-up is planned.

He commented that over the years, he is finding women to be more and more aggressive. "Lots of women are more overt. I am not a heavy pusher, so it works for me."

—Larry– 75 – Twice Divorced —

You are going to meet Larry again, later on, in the chapter on "Money, Money, Money." Larry was my late husband's college roommate and best friend.

We are sitting at his kitchen table, sipping a cup of coffee in Scottsdale, Arizona. Larry was a senior partner in a major law firm in New York. He was married for twenty years, got divorced, re-married, but then got divorced again.

Larry is now seventy-five years old, and in very good shape. He stands tall and straight. He was always big-boned and that has served him well. He appears as strong as an ox, even though his lower back has been giving him grief for a number of years. He dyes whatever is left of his hair black, and it becomes him. His face is quite unlined. His features are strong. In short, Larry is still a pleasure to look at!

Although Larry insisted that he was still practicing his law profession, when pushed with my questioning he admitted he didn't really have many clients left. If any clients.

I spied several rows of pictures of women attached with scotch tape to the wall next to the kitchen table. Next to each picture was taped a hand-written 3x5" card with the woman's personal data—her age, her body type, and a few other details. I asked Larry what that was all about.

Larry told me that these were the possible dates he had culled from two different dating sites. Typical of what I knew of Larry as a thorough researcher in law, he was applying his thorough research skills to dating.

I sleep late every morning, until about 9:30 a.m. Usually, I keep nothing in the house. So I get into my car and drive to a local breakfast shop. On the way,

I buy a newspaper. I sit alone at the counter. Heck, you never know who might walk in and sit down next to you.

I linger around and return home around 10:30 or 11:00. If I have an errand or two to run—like the dry cleaners or something—I might return around noon. But I am rarely running around in Scottsdale in the afternoon. It's too damn hot.

I turn on the computer and check for email. That takes me about a half hour or so.

Finally, around two o'clock, my workday begins.

"Workday?" I ask.

Yes. Dating is work! I am on two dating sites. One is a dating site for seniors presumably over fifty. The other is just a general dating site. Those 3x5" cards you see posted on this wall are the present configuration detailing my interest in them. I move them around as I connect with the women.

If I actually do meet any of these postings, I take them off this wall, staple their card to another card, and write down memorable items of the meeting. Like what they really look like in person, their weight, their age, and what I actually find out about them.

(He smiles). It can be very embarrassing if you mix information up. Trust me, until I developed this system, I'd mix women up. Big time! There was the time I had a second date with the wrong woman!

It also works wonders for a second date. The woman is always impressed that I remembered so much about them. So I get "boy-scout" points for my attentiveness. They even tell me that they are impressed with my memory. (He smiles again.)

I scan these websites for new prospects every day. Sometimes I send a flirt. Sometimes I don't. My complaint for these websites is that I found it hard to save my searches. Sometimes, I return and decide to make contact with someone I came across, but cannot find her again. So now I am taking more notes by hand as I scan.

Lately, I've been expanding my search to other states. Don't know why.

"Larry," I ask, "don't you get bored with this repetitive dating?"

Eleanor, I am lonely, and have been lonely for a couple of years now. Internet dating is the most efficient and cheapest way I can meet a woman. Yes, it's repetitive. Yes, it's boring. Yes, I am pretty sick of this. But it's the best I can do.

"Larry, have you actually met any woman who you wanted to see more of? Who you wanted to continue dating?"

Yes, I have. But that's another story.

Yes, dear reader, it is another story. You will meet Larry again in, "Money, Money, Money."

POST 65-YEAR-OLD WIDOWS AND DIVORCEES
VIEW THEIR SINGLE DATING LIFE DIFFERENTLY

Single people who have become single in their later lives have come to be called "Silver Singles." This expression has been attached more to women than men. Here, we are talking more about women who have become single in their sixties, seventies, and eighties.

I found that there was generally a large difference in how these later-life single women viewed their dating depending on whether they re-entered the dating world as a widow or as a divorcee. In general, I found later-life divorced women to be much more bitter about their new state of singleness than the widows. There was residual anger over their state of being a divorcee in her sixties, seventies, and eighties.

In general, they see themselves as less desirable. They see themselves as "damaged goods." They see the fact that they are older in the singles world as a deterrent to forming a new relationship. They are angry that they are at a disadvantage. They believe that their age works against them. They feel less attractive. They think they are less able to attract a man of "appropriate age." When a date doesn't work out, or when a relationship doesn't form or work out, they become more loathe than widows of the same age to try again.

Among the silver divorcees, there are those women, albeit a small minority, who were the instigators of the divorce over sixty. In general, they said they only wished they had done it earlier. They had the special strength to take the initiative because they were driven to it by their husband's abusive conduct: Their husbands were alcoholics and they couldn't take it anymore. Their husbands were cheating, and they couldn't take it anymore.

But despite their personal strength, they voiced the same lack of self-confidence when they faced re-entering into the world of singles past the age of sixty: All the men out there are looking only for younger women. They were giving up, believing it was too late to "start over."

In general, the divorcees in their sixties, seventies, and eighties, whether they were the instigator or not, insisted they knew that older single men wanted someone younger. Divorcees, coping with the fact of being divorced after sixty-five, were most likely to lie about their age.

The widows, on the whole, are happier and more positive about meeting a new man. They do not see dating in their sixties, seventies, and eighties as "starting over" but more as a continuation of life. They carry no wounds from their past relationship. Not one widow ever said to me she had a lousy marriage. Or she had a poor marriage. What's the point? It's over and they've forgotten the bad times. Or if they haven't actually forgotten, they do not let it color their new life going forward.

Because of their different mindset, widows are less worried about their appearance, less worried about making a first impression, less worried about not looking like a thirty-five-year-old. They see that relationships over sixty-five are built on more factors than just youthful appearance. They're more likely to seek other types of compatibility.

— Jackie – Divorced Twice —

Jacklyn was a stewardess for a prominent airline. At seventy-seven years old, you can still see her good looks. She keeps herself slim. She is fashionably dressed. Her face is relatively unlined. She speaks with animation and sparkle. She is clearly attractive now, as she must have been when she was young.

Her second husband asked for a divorce after fifteen years of marriage. He was sixty-eight at the time. She was sixty-five years old at the time.

What did he blame? Jackie said he blamed her for drinking too much. She blamed the fact that he started having affairs in his sixties.

When asked if she thought she was drinking too much, Jackie responded with, "Life had become so freakin' boring."

She claims to meet new men easily and often. Sometimes they are younger than she. Sometimes they are older. "There are plenty of fish in the sea," Jackie says.

But when our conversation turns specifically to her dating experiences, her sparkly demeanor turns sour.

"Lots of men out there, but they add up to one big zero."

"What makes you say that?" I ask.

Then she begins her litany of problems with dating. I will distill some of them here:

"Wayne's kids kept getting in the way. He spent too much time with them."

"When John learned my real age, he dropped me like a hot potato."

"Zac couldn't be trusted. He kept ogling younger women."

"Most of the men refuse to spend money on me. I am high maintenance."

"How did men get so ugly all of a sudden?"

"I really deserve a younger man, but I don't have enough money for him."

Jackie is currently out of the dating scene. She simply looked at me, and said, "I've had enough of these losers."

I left our interview thinking that Jackie would stay out of the dating scene for a while, but someday, in a few months perhaps, she'd be drawn back in—like a moth is drawn to a flame. Jackie keeps herself much too feminine and attractive to really want to end that part of her life. In my opinion, it would be better if Jackie admitted that to herself. She would be a lot happier in her new world.

— Michael – Divorced at 72 —

Michael is eighty-four years old. Michael is every bit a dating senior. He checks his Internet singles website often. He is a relatively well-established author of novels. He teaches courses occasionally on writing at a variety of schools in the metropolitan area. He stated unequivocally that an intelligent woman is very sexy—no matter her age or physical appearance—that is, to a point.

Michael is divorced. After forty-five years of marriage, his wife simply wanted to call it quits. So at the ripe age of seventy-two, Michael "parachuted" back into the singles world.

Michael stated his dating experience has led him to prefer widows over divorcees.

When he goes online to check out a profile, he considers "widow" as a plus.

"Widows tend to be less sharp."

"Widows are giving. More negotiable. They are used to compromise."

"I am very set in my ways," says Michael, "so I need to have the other person more the giver in my relationship."

Michael kept coming back to the point that it was a woman's mind that turned him on, rather than her physical attributes. So he does not care if she has gray hair, blonde hair, blue hair, whatever. He does not care if she is skinny or fat.

I am too old to feel sexually attracted on first sight...just because she is a female. The chemistry is there, of course, but my real attraction comes when I am talking to her, listening to her, and looking in her eyes.

After that, when it comes to continuing our relationship and bonding, I find the widows more willing to come into my world. For example, what movie should we see. What food to eat. Places to travel to.

I confess I am quite settled in my ways. After all, I am in my eighties. What do you expect? (he asks rhetorically).

It's too much of a hassle to date a divorcee when I can date a more pliable widow.

— Wanda – Divorced at 68 —

I woke up one day when I was sixty-seven years old, looked over at the man I had been living with for twenty years, and said to myself, "I got to get outta here, no matter what." I couldn't stand his snoring another minute. I couldn't stand the way he moved, he ate, everything he said. It was as if a switch was turned off. I can't explain it. It may have been because our kids were grown up and gone from the house. It may have been because he retired around that time and was around the house all the time. It may have been because he was fat and ugly, and I suddenly noticed it. But all I can say is that there was no turning back.

I lived with those feeling for about six months, and then suddenly said, "I want a divorce." Just like the movies. (She half-smiled at that comment.) Financial issues were not much of a problem. Everything was paid off. I wanted to move out and leave everything behind. And that's what pretty much happened.

And I am living to regret it. This singles world is crappy. I'm lonely, maybe more, or just as lonely as I was married. Dating is hard work, if not impossible. The world is made for couples. I still don't like going out with other women. I certainly don't like doing anything with other women.

There may be lots of men out there. Or at least that's what they tell me. But where are the good ones? They are no better than my ex-husband. And they all seem to want younger women. If I tell them I am fifty-eight, they come calling. If I tell them I am sixty-eight, they turn away. That is, until they meet me. So I have to lie at the outset. Something I was brought up not to do. The fact is I look pretty damn good for sixty-eight. Most folks take ten years off my age when they are guessing. So I think of it as a white lie. No harm done.

I've also been lying and saying on the Internet that I am a widow. That's almost harder to live with. My ex is very much alive, and we do have to communicate with each other because of our kids and finances. But I think men prefer to date widows. Correct me if you found this to be a wrong assumption.

I know you are changing my name for the book. I am on the Internet. And I am lying.

So life has been a trade-off for me. I expect to live another twenty or so years. I am still young enough to hope the best is yet to come.

— Patricia – 78 – Divorcee —

Don't you ever dare say to me that I am over the hill. I'm the "foxiest" septuagenarian you'd ever want to meet. I started getting rid of my lousy bastard of a husband just as soon as my kids were out of town, with lives of their own. It took almost four years for me to get that divorce. I did pretty well. Got the house, alimony, and use of our beach house. I finally can control my own destiny. Being where I am now, financially independent, not having to answer to that bastard, was worth the ups and downs of my new dating world. Yes, it's pretty rough. But I am a survivor. I survived a lousy marriage. The singles world is a piece of cake in comparison. Men like me. I am funny. Life is too serious. I like to laugh, and make others laugh. There is always a twinkle in my eye, no matter how I slept the night before. What happens in my private world of health, appearance, and emotions stays in my private world. I am not interested in a man's problems, or his health, or even his financial condition. I just want a good time until I check in with the great almighty.

At the time of the interview, Patricia had been divorced for eight years. She got divorced at seventy years old. If you think of the singles world over sixty-five years old as one fraught with danger and disappointments, then you've got to say Patricia is a survivor.

Patricia just might be one of the silver singles' "exception that proves the rule."

You will meet Patricia again in Chapter 5, "Mortality and Other Discomforts."

There are many more dating stories I could tell. So many of the folks I interviewed had so much in common. Yet each single senior's dating story was unique in its own way.

You will have your own story to tell.

***

WHo WouLd HAVE THougHT THAt I'd GEt MY SEcoNd WiNd At 75!!!

CHAPTER THREE
SEX AND THE SINGLE SENIOR

WHY IS IT THAT WHENEVER I TELL ANY PERSON, young or old, male or female—anyone—that I am writing a book called, "Secrets of Dating and Mating After Medicare," they crack a big smile—even laugh? The young or the old, the male or the female, then tells me he or she wants to read the book, or buy the book for his mom, or for her dad, her brother, his sister, and so on. If everyone who responded this way actually does buy this book, I can tell you I have a bestseller on my hands.

But. I wonder why their first reaction is a laugh. If I told them the title of my book was "Secrets of Dating and Mating After **50**," I am willing to bet they would have had no reaction whatsoever. A single person in his or her fifties of course is expected to be "out there" dating and mating.

Our society, meaning you, me, media, government—everyone—looks at a sixty-five-year-old plus as "winding down" and "over the hill." Judging by folks' reaction to my title, my writing a book that states we are dating and mating, and even more, that we might even have "secrets" about it, is still considered odd enough to bring about a smile or a laugh.

Being over the hill at sixty-five was never true. But now, we are coming out of the closet (to use the expression) into the mainstream of life. We are flexing our muscles, literally and figuratively. We are skiing. We are running marathons. We are playing senior tennis and senior golf. We are traveling. We are hiking. You, my dear reader, may want to state a few activities of your own.

We are in an anti-aging revolution for older folks, for folks after Medicare...over sixty-five years old. Nothing makes that fact clearer than a description of our sexual needs and desires. This is the book that brings that truism home. And this is the chapter that lays it all out for us to understand.

OUR SEXUAL REVOLUTION

There are three major reasons for this sexual revolution for the post-Medicare generations. 1: Increasing male longevity. 2: Senior sexuality and its growing social acceptance. And 3: the Internet in all its ramifications—as the great communicator—allowing unlimited interaction between all people, at any age.

OUR DRIVE TO DATE AND MATE

You read in the previous chapter that dating is possible at an older age because more men are living into their 70s, 80s, and 90s. You read there is a much greater pool of senior men out there. It's a different dating world from Pearl's world. You do not need to show up at the grave and attack the grieving widower.

In this chapter, we are looking behind the scenes, under the covers, so to speak, of what drives so many of us to want to date at this late age. Why are we willing to spend a great amount of time? Why do we expend a great amount of mental and physical energy? Why do we expend money, even lots of money, simply to meet someone? What is driving us to dating and mating just as we are getting older, slowing down, retiring, feeling worse, and facing our own mortality?

OUR SEX DRIVE IS WITH US OUR ENTIRE LIVES

The other day, my guy—eighty-two years old—and I were sitting in my living room, watching a Netflix movie. We both looked at each other and said, almost simultaneously...why do we feel differently, sitting here, male and female, watching a movie we could be seeing with someone of our own sex? Watching the movie was a part of spending our evening together, talking about the same small things, things we pretty much could talk about with anyone else of our own sex. Gossip, stories, family, comments, and the like. Yet we agreed the feeling was different. We both laughed and admitted that while the activity might be the same, our underlying feelings were different. There was hardly any physical contact, and no active sexual contact. Yet we felt sexually connected. We just knew we were connected by some sort of sexual energy.

No matter how old we are, we have the need to be with a person with whom we share sexual energy. Whether we decide to actively pursue this need is a decision that older folks (and younger folks, to be fair) make independently of that feeling.

Psychological discovery and description of our sexual feelings should be attributed to one person—Sigmund Freud. Freud was a psychiatrist in the late 19th-early 20th century. He died in 1939. He has been credited with the founding of psychoanalysis.

Freud identified and described our sexual nature. In no uncertain terms, he gives credence to the theory that the human psyche is hard-wired for sexual energy—meaning that it is with us from birth until the day we die.

Freud provided a structural model of our psyche. He said we have a conscious and a sub-conscious. Our conscious is composed of the cognitive—our thought processes. We are aware of our conscious. We can hear ourselves think. According to Freud, our conscious makes up a very small part of who we are. At any given time, we are only aware of a very small part of what makes up our personality; most of what we are is buried and inaccessible.

Freud named this buried part of our psyche the "sub-conscious." Our sub-conscious is composed of our emotional processes.

Freud believed that the majority of what we experience in our lives, the underlying emotions, beliefs, feelings, and impulses, are not available to us at a conscious level. He believed that what drives us is buried in our unconscious. Although buried, they continued to impact us dramatically.

Freud used the words "id," "ego," and "super-ego" as three theoretical constructs that describe the activity and interaction of our mental life. He popularized the hypothesis that the id, ego, and super-ego are the three parts of the psychic apparatus of humankind. Our *id* is where we store our uncoordinated, instinctual desires, our need for instant gratification; our super-ego stores our critical and moralizing role, where we make judgments; our *ego* is the rational, cognitive part of our psyche, where we organize our thoughts and mediate between our *id* and *super-ego*.

Here, we are interested in discussing the *id*, or more precisely, what Freud referred to as the *Libido*, a part of the *id*. The *Libido,* according to Freud, is part of our psyche, at a very basic level, and furnishes us our sexual desire and urges. As part of our sub-conscious, we function without being intellectually aware of how our sexual desires and urges actually work.

The word "Libido" was not manufactured by Freud but comes from the Latin. Libido in Latin means "desire, longing fancy, or lust." Although the adjective "libidinous," meaning "lustful," has been used in English for 500 or so years, "libido" only entered the language in 1913, thanks to Freud and other psychoanalysts who applied the term to psychic energy or drive, and especially to the sexual instinct.

Freud believed that the energy of the sexual drive was a component of the life instinct. Our sex drive cannot be directly observed, but it is there, within us at every age. Our sex drive is with us all the time. Our sex drive can be stimulated, excited, and set in motion by stimuli. It can also be controlled. But it cannot be eliminated.

Freud emphasized in all his writings that the human being is born with his/her sex drive and it stays with the person until death.

What was lost in translation over the years is whether or not this sexual drive component loses its power as the person ages. In short, although we are born with sexual energy (meaning it is developed during our infancy), do we lose it, as we might lose our hearing, our vision, even our mind?

If we look at the cultural patterns of our society over the ages, society seemed to have thought older men did not lose their sexual drive. The chastity belt was worn by the young woman in the Middle Ages. Older women did not wear chastity belts. There was the common thought that the old(er) woman did not need a chastity belt because she did not experience any longing or would not be desirable by men. On the other hand, however, literature shows lots of examples of men's "virility" at old(er) ages. Older men who could and did impregnate women were looked up to and admired.

Importantly, societal attitudes toward sexual activity for those over fifty were either scorned or considered to be nonexistent. As late as the 1950s, women (and men, to be fair) were not even considered to be sexually active, or sexually interesting.

Alfred Kinsey has been acknowledged as the founder of "sexology," the study of sexual behavior. Among other things, he wrote two books, "Sexual Behavior in the Human Male," published in 1948, and "Sexual Behavior in the Human Female," published 1953. Both books make for an interesting read (if you like data entries and data studies), both for what they say and don't say.

For example, Kinsey included contact with erogenous zones, such as breast fondling, as sexual activity in addition to actual intercourse.

However, what is most interesting and disturbing was his sample population. Kinsey and his group interviewed over 5,300 males, and 5,900 females. Kinsey elected not to interview anyone over fifty. Not one of these more than 10,000 folks were over fifty years old. He and his team simply believed that folks over fifty had no sexual drive.

If Kinsey were to do his studies today, he would do well to interview folks well into their seventies, eighties, and nineties.

To put it succinctly, Freud was proved to be right. We are sexually hard-wired from birth to death. There is sexuality today, among the early old, middle old, and yes, the old old folk out here and there. What we do about it, how we handle it, is a matter of choice. "Choice" is my all-encompassing term which includes our mindset, our emotional makeup, our fears, our expectations, our background, our belief system, and any other word or concept that comes to your mind that affects your sexual conduct.

SOCIETY IS CATCHING UP

Society has become more tolerant of older folks' sexual conversations and activities.

Not only has society become more tolerant of older folks' sexuality, but it has become BIG BUSINESS.

For example: our AARP Bulletin. Do you know anyone over sixty-five years old who does not receive the Bulletin?

The AARP Bulletin is chock full of information aimed at the senior: Settling an Estate; Your Nest Egg; articles on Cataracts, Vitamin D and Blood Pressure, and Glaucoma.

Look at the full-page ads—just the big, full-page ads for now. Thumbing through a recent issue of the AARP Bulletin, here is what you might see:

There are full-page ads for a cell phone product, for a high-quality TV and radio sound system, for a couple of auto insurance companies, a medical alert system credit card come-on, TV satellite dish; a new type of hearing aid life insurance (but not if you are over eighty), a computer specially designed for you, and "not your grandchildren," and then suddenly there appears a full-page ad for DVDs: "SEX VIDEOS."

My guy and I were sitting around the living room. I forget what he was doing, but I was going through the day's mail. I was skimming my AARP Bulletin, and hit upon the ad. I read it aloud to my guy. "Honey, how about my getting the video, 'SEX, it's never too late to learn something new.'" It tells us to order the sex video, and we get 50% off the three sex videos and receive three more videos.

We were both a bit embarrassed at the thought...at first. But then we both realized, here was an ad in a forum we trusted. It could not be porn. We needed to be a bit more broad-minded about it.

So I did order it. It was the first time in my life that I actually did something like this.

Conversations dealing with sex are coming into the open, and into the living rooms of older Americans.

<u>Another example, one you should remember:</u> the Bob Dole commercial? Not a model, Bob Dole was nothing less than our Republican heartland (from Kansas) presidential opponent to Bill Clinton in 1996. To whom he lost.

Shortly after he lost the election, our country was treated to Bob Dole in a new way. Bob went public in a TV advertisement with three words or phrases, never before heard in public, much less from a presidential aspirant. The words were "prostate cancer," "Viagra," and "erectile dysfunction"—ED, as the pharmaceutical companies like to call it.

Bob Dole was seventy-five years old when he made that commercial, when he spoke to the nation of his personal desire to be youthful, vigorous, and vital again.

For seniors, for whom Bob Dole became a sexual spokesman, it was coming out of the closet.

You will bump into Bob Dole again in chapter 4, "Mortality and Other Discomforts."

We seniors are sexy. We have sexual needs. We have sexual demands. We are hard-wired that way. And it's perfectly acceptable!

The renewal and enhancement of sexual energy at every age has become big, big business. Both sexes are spending money like water. This appears to be worldwide.

I spied an article in the *Wall Street Journal*: "Lip Service: A Hair-Raising Procedure Grows in Turkey." It has become a billion-dollar business in Turkey, not chump change for a not-so-rich economy. Facial hair transplant is at the fringe of a broader healthcare tourism boom in Turkey, which last year generated over a billion dollars in revenue.

In Middle Eastern society, full mustaches are a sign of virility. A Northern Iranian businessman said he traveled to a Turkish doctor's surgery clinic after years of low self-esteem over the patchy hair grown on his upper lip.

American society has become very comfortable with hair transplants for our men. Witness our ex-Vice President, Joe Biden.

MEN

Senior men are taking erection-producing drugs. "Natural supplements" such as Enzyte 14/7, Nite Rider, and Maxaman promise to enhance erection quality, arousal, and response. There are many creams on the market, found in our everyday, main street drugstores, as well as lubricants like the K-Y series promising to make the sexual experience better for both sexes.

Senior men are also undergoing insertion of penile pumps, medically called penile prosthesis. Medicare paid for, I want you to know. A popular kind today is a hydraulic inflatable insert that allows a man to have an erection whenever he chooses, simply by pumping his scrotum up. It does not affect his ability to ejaculate, and men are claiming to once again experience the "Full Monty."

Some men continue to reach for ejaculation...explaining that they feel frustrated, unrequited, and inadequate if they do not ejaculate. Yet other men say it is no longer necessary that they need to "perform" in order to feel fulfilled. Their answers ranged from their pleasure in seeing their women partners are happy from their touch to their pleasure in women going down on them and giving them blowjobs.

— Joe —

Joe, who was very forthcoming in his interview, said that he believed the only way he could sincerely satisfy a woman was to be able to penetrate her. That was the only way, he felt, sex would be fulfilling to a woman. So, at seventy-nine, he tells me how good he feels to be able to please his girlfriend. He was taking Viagra for years, but has recently had a penile pump inserted into his scrotum. He claims it was the healthier thing to do because it did not affect his "chemical makeup."

— Roland —

Roland is eighty-six. He looks every bit of it. Whatever hair he has left is stark white. Lined face. Much too heavy. He looks as if he hasn't moved around in years. He has trouble walking. Yet when he started answering my questions about his sex life, his face lit up. Color came to his skin. He suddenly looked ten years younger.

"I've had a girlfriend for five years now. I know how to keep her happy. She knows how to keep me happy. We had to work on it. It took time. It took honesty. But she wanted it as badly as I wanted it."

He continued, "I am not so sure that she is as sexually needy as I am. She travels more, alone, to see her family. She has more outside interests than I do. I am more sedentary than she is. But she always comes back to me."

I ask "Why?" Roland smiles again, and says, "I don't really know. She probably feels my loyalty, my need for her. She probably feels my love. You'd have to ask her about the rest."

Roland described his girlfriend as out of shape as well. But he said with a great smile that she had big "tits." Big tits never go out of shape!

I never did meet his girlfriend. But I understand they are still a couple.

— Greg —

Greg is a retired book editor. He is quite proud of his editorial achievements, having been a senior editor at a major publishing house in New York City for more than twenty years.

Now, at eighty-six, he is clearly a shadow of himself...or of what he must have been. He is hard of hearing. Although he was wearing a hearing aid, he seemed not to be benefiting much from it—as far as I could tell. He is rather handsome. Good strong features. But he clearly has trouble walking. He is bent over. His height must have been over six feet, but now he is severely bowed over, reducing his height to maybe 5'9".

Greg was never married.

We met in an odd way. It got around my apartment building, where I lived at the time, that I was writing a book. Somewhere, somehow, I was told that there was a book editor, a rather eminent retired book editor, who was living in my building. So I got up my gumption and contacted him. I said that I was writing a book, and would he be kind enough to look at one of my chapters and comment about it? He was very kind and said he would be glad to.

That's when I found out he was over sixty-five and single, making him a part of my target population for this book. I asked if I could interview him.

Of all my interviewees, Greg was the most insistent, even vehement, in his attitude to sex and relationships.

Greg insisted that he has a sexual relationship with a woman even though they barely kiss, never hold hands, and have never gone any further than that. Greg stated that a woman's intellectual make-up is sexy to him. He referred to Betty, a woman he has been involved with for the past eight years. Betty is seventy-six now. She met him when she was sixty-eight years old, and he was eighty. She lives in his neighborhood, and they get together every day...or almost every day. She has never slept over.

I try to say that maybe they are just good friends, but Greg cuts me off. They are so intellectually compatible, says Greg, that he can feel the chemistry between them. Betty is his aphrodisiac (his word, not mine). "To me," says Greg, "there is nothing more sexy, more seductive, more sexually satisfying than an intelligent woman."

I wonder what Freud might say to Greg's story.

— Fred —

"It's never too late to have a happy childhood," says Fred in answer to my question about his sexual relations at his age of eighty-three.

Fred shows every bit of his age. He is, of course, almost bald. But as he admitted to me, he dyes whatever fringe he has left. It makes him feel stronger. Please note, he did not use the word "younger." It was clear from our meeting there was no way he could look younger. He has arthritis of the hands. His fingers are gnarled. He had cataracts removed a few years ago, at the age of seventy-nine, so his sight is pretty good. His face is lined with wrinkles. He is very paunchy—a description you, the reader, might say is a politically correct way of saying "fat." He has stomach troubles and must be very picky about what he eats, and when.

Yet despite all this, Fred describes himself as a very sexy guy:

My idol is Nelson Rockefeller. Now there's a guy who lived until he died. Cowboys, you might say, want to die with their boots on. Well, this urban guy wants to die with his pants off!

My wife and I were divorced after thirty-five years of marriage. We were both in our late sixties. I've been having a great time ever since. I have had at least seven girlfriends. When they see that I refuse to get more serious, they break up with me. Then I'm on to the next. It may take a couple of months, but there's a lot of gals out there. I am not that picky, you know. As you can see, I can't be that picky.

I don't remember when I had so much fun. It must have been in my teens. That's when "it" (meaning his penis, of course) was up so much, I couldn't keep it down! Well, maybe I'm exaggerating a bit. At times it was very frustrating. All the energy, and no one to sink it into. (He smiled as he said this.)

Sure, I'm not the stud I was in my teens. I still do get a rise once in a while. And I still do ejaculate once in a while. But I treat it as a challenge. Hell, I have so few challenges left in my life. I'm retired. I live on a set income. I see no financial challenges ahead of me. I no longer can play any sport—am too arthritic. So what's left? My sex drive. My sport today, my one and only sport today, is having sex, as best as I can.

I watch as much porn as I can, without seeming to be a freak. I wander between supplements. You name it and I've probably tried it. I have not had any surgical help, but there's always next year.

I don't need to prove I can have kids. I don't need to prove I can make a woman come. For the older woman, I figure that's her problem.

It's really more about the challenge, than the result.

And that's the end of my story.

WOMEN

Not one woman over sixty-five has said to me that she must have intercourse to feel sexually fulfilled. Nor do they use the word "sex" literally, the way the men do. As a group, they were not as forthcoming about their need for intercourse or sexual contact in the same way that men were. Each woman has explained that she believes the foreplay, or the thought of foreplay, the closeness and touch of her guy's flesh, even handholding can be as much as she needs to feel sexually fulfilled. As it turned out, however, senior women are certainly into use of enhancements to establish and ensure their sexual attractiveness to men.

Women have been using everything available to enhance their attractiveness from time immemorial. You do not need to have been a student of history to know the story of Cleopatra and her seduction of Mark Antony. But did you know that Cleopatra perfumed the sails of her ships as her regatta met Mark Antony in the harbor? Did you know she used what we call cosmetic enhancements—blush, lipstick, powder—on her face and body? She dyed her hair and eyebrows. Her clothes were provocative.

But what about older women? Women past their prime? Women no longer of child-bearing age? (Remember, the words old, older, and senior refer to a different chronological age depending on our changing longevity. You will read more about this in Chapter 4, "Mortality and Other Discomforts.")

There was a time when a woman was considered too old to undergo facial plastic surgery. My mother-in-law had a facelift when she was sixty years old. Then, some fifteen years later, she went back to the same surgeon for another facelift. He refused, saying she was too old. This was in the 1990s.

According to John E. Sherman, a prominent plastic surgeon, whom I interviewed for the book, the number of women older than seventy undergoing "a facelift" has increased. He attributed this fact to improved medical advances on how to treat an "aging" face, to people's better health in their later years, and to the increased demand from women in their seventies, eighties, and nineties.

It used to be (feels like a long, long time ago), plastic surgery was the major and almost only way for women to reset their physical clocks. Now a woman has so many dermatological procedures to choose from, it is impossible to describe them all, or to even keep track.

Botox, of course, is one, but now only one of a myriad of procedures. Women have creams and serums promising to get rid of those wrinkles, to bring back our long eyelashes, to get rid of that cellulose.

I, myself, am fascinated with the growing power of Internet offerings from purveyors of beauty deals like Groupon. I am being offered discount deals for revitalizing and beautifying parts of my body that I never knew existed.

Catering to the sexuality of seniors is no longer a taboo, or behind closed doors.

Freud was right. Business has latched on to it. Medicine and marketing to seniors is growing by leaps and bounds. Senior women are using enhancements to establish and enhance their attractiveness, their allure, in increasing numbers. I have not come across any firm statistics on how much older women spend on youth-enhancing and allure-enhancing products. But if the number of ads for products and services to revitalize "aging" skin, to bring back a youthful figure, to reset our clocks, is any indication of senior usage and senior financial clout, then we are a formidable, active group.

— Peggy —

Peggy tells me she has been going to a wellness doctor for years. "What is a wellness doctor?" I ask. Peggy says a regular doctor takes care of special issues, like heart, stomach, skin, etc. A wellness doctor takes care of the whole person. I say, "Peggy, this is a question of your sexuality at seventy-two years old. So where are we going with this conversation?"

Peggy stated she had a pellet inserted under her skin for a number of years. The pellet is a combination of testosterone, estrogen, and progesterone. It lasts about three months. She stated that she went to a wellness doctor because she felt very sluggish and depressed. But other doctors (cardiologist, gynecologist, internist, etc.) checked her out, and said she was fine. In desperation, she went to a wellness doctor.

After the insertion, Peggy stated she felt almost an immediate change. She had more energy, more positive attitude to life. And also, she felt more sexually aroused on a day-to-day basis.

After my conversation with Peggy, I researched this treatment. Yes, it does purport to improve the "libido." Remember the word "libido?" You came across it earlier in this chapter, when we talked about Freud.

Actually, Peggy was still married at the time when she started her wellness treatment. She started it in her late fifties. Today, she is widowed. But at seventy-two, she claims to have the sexual energy of a twenty-year-old. And is loving it. We stopped our interview right there.

— **Barbara** —

Barbara is the only female senior whom I am including who never married. She claims to have had a few long-term relationships (over ten years), so I decided to include her. But in all fairness, that might account for her present acceptance of her aging. Barbara looks and acts every bit of her age: seventy. Yet she is never without a relationship. So I asked her how and why she seemed to want to be in a relationship. Her answer was simply, "Everything is done by and for twos." That is true. Man (including woman, of course, as well) is a social animal. Man wants and needs company.

Barbara then went on, "So I have to pay the price."

"Meaning?" I asked.

"Meaning," she said, "I have to be sexually active. That means I go down on my guys. I caress them. I make love to them. That's all I will do. I do not spread my legs." Then she smiled a bit and said, "I am not even sure I could spread my legs." She stated she did no exercise. She actually expressed loathing at the thought of doing exercise. "I don't even walk if I can help it. I take taxis or shared rides everywhere."

"Don't the men complain?" I asked. Barbara explained that she has always found a man who is in sync with her. That's all he wants. It's enough for him. So she develops a harmonious relationship until illness or something else separates the companionship part. The last guy she had (she did not even give him a name) had a serious of personal and family misfortunes. He broke his leg. Then he broke his arm. Then he had his hip replaced. Someone in his family got ill and he spent time with his familial obligations. Barbara said, "That's when I broke up with him. He was no longer as available to me as I wanted. So, it was sayonara and on to the next," she said, with a small wave of her hand. "Sayonara" means "goodbye" in Japanese.

— Sarah —

Sarah is obese. There is no other way to describe her. She confessed to weighing 185 lbs. She is 5'5" tall. She is seventy-five, and she is diabetic.

Sarah never married. But she lived with a partner for eighteen years, and had a daughter with him. Her daughter is now in her forties, married with two children of her own. Her daughter is also obese, according to Sarah.

Sarah has a boyfriend of six years. They do not live together. She described him as also heavyset. But, "he is not a drinker, not a smoker. A good man."

Sex is great and often, says Sarah. The position they use is her on top of him. She needs lubricant, and so does he. She thinks he uses Viagra or something else to aid him in an erection, but she didn't know what he does when he is preparing for his visit.

She does not experience orgasms. But she doesn't tell him, one way or another. And he does not ask. She said she needs the physical contact, because it makes her feel loved, like nothing else could.

Her attitude to sex is quite lighthearted. She commented that sex with her boyfriend is the best entertainment she can think of. It's cheap. It's engrossing. It's active. It's downright fun. Her last comment to me on this subject was, "We almost broke my bed once."

— Victoria —

Vickie was widowed when she was sixty-eight years old. It was a long marriage of more than forty years. Vickie had four children. Three survived. She has nine grandchildren ranging in age from post college down to sub-teenagers. Her husband was financially successful. They had three homes, and belonged to two country clubs. Vickie and her husband kept themselves physically trim and active.

Vickie spoke a bit about her feelings of "parachuting back in" to the dating world after her husband's death. Like me, her dating began easily after her husband's death. Because she had an active life, was physically attractive, with many friends, she was introduced by mutual friends and acquaintances to new men.

Vickie said she felt like a virgin when she started dating again. When her date French-kissed her (inserted his tongue into her mouth), she was so taken back, she laughed, covered her mouth, and said, "Wow," all almost simultaneously. She went on to say:

I get more pleasure out of sex now than when I was younger. When I met Jake, I would feel all tingly when he touched me. I even giggled at times. He was in his eighties, and was unable to have an erection, even with Viagra. But he was so loving to me. He kept the lights on while he caressed my body. I kept my eyes closed. I don't know why. I guess I just couldn't feel comfortable with my eyes open. I think I was still embarrassed by my naked exposure in front of a strange man. But despite my closed eyes, I could tell he enjoyed looking at me, submissive under his touch. He emoted loving sounds, and words here and there. I was silent. I imagined myself on a beach, naked.

His touch on my body, his caresses to my nipples, were the light trade winds I remembered from my husband and our many Caribbean vacations together.

I came easily. It was a clitoral orgasm, obviously. After that I went down on him. I don't remember ever going down on my husband even once in our 44 years together. And here I was, doing that to a relatively strange man!

"Did he ask you to go down on him?"

No. It just came naturally to me. I wanted to please him. I may have even asked him whether he was enjoying it. I wasn't sure if I was doing it right.

Despite his flaccidity, he ejaculated. I remember he said he was "in heaven" and "this is heaven" and other similar expressions of pleasure. I appreciated those comments. It made me feel good. I think it added to my sexual pleasure.

I was surprised. I had no idea a man could be soft, and then suddenly ejaculate. Looking back, he did get a bit harder just before he ejaculated. But at the time I was comparing him to my husband. My husband in his younger days was already hard when he approached me in bed. So he was ready, willing, and able to have intercourse. Our love-making was more perfunctory. He caressed me very briefly. I remember a kiss or two. Then it was "Wham, bam, thank you ma'am."

With Jake, sex felt like a new experience. Exhilarating. We used to giggle in bed, and said to each other that we felt like teenagers. I remember saying how naughty I felt.

"Are you still with him?" I asked.

No. We were a couple for three years. Then he got cancer of the blood. Our bonding continued to be there, except it was in hand-holding, and in other demonstrative ways. He died a few years ago.

"And now?" I asked.

I have a new boyfriend, Wayne. Who is actually a bit younger than I am. I am now eighty-one. He is seventy-eight. Wayne and I have been together for about three years now.

"Do you want to make any comment about you with your two boyfriends after your long marriage to one man?"

Wayne is a totally different type of lover from Jake. But thanks to Jake, I am also a more relaxed sexual giver and taker. It is more important for Wayne to ejaculate inside of me. Obviously, Jake was beyond that need. Wayne may have taken Viagra or some other enhancement, but when he met me, he was off everything. Wayne also is a wonderful lover. He takes his time caressing me. He tells me he loves "tits." Sometimes I wonder whether his love of tits is his newfound interest, in his later and single life, as my love of going down on my lover is my newfound interest in my later and single life.

I say to Vickie, "This book is not being written necessarily as a guidebook or a guideline for sex in our senior years. I simply am trying to explain the current landscape for single seniors, in the hope they will take something positive and hopeful from it. But since you are so explicit, is there something you might want to say to our readers?"

My advice to all the women out there. Enjoy yourselves. Allow yourself to get to know men all over again. In every way.

Come to think of it, I would give the same advice to the men reading this book. Enjoy yourselves. Allow yourself to get to know women all over again. In every way.

Simple, perhaps, but this advice rings true. So I am passing it on to you, dear reader.

***

KING ARTHUR, 76 YEARS OLD,
OFFERS YOU HIS UNCENSORED STORY.
HE WAS MARRIED FOR 44 YEARS,
HAS TWO GROWN CHILDREN, AND
THREE GRANDCHILDREN.

CHAPTER FOUR

KING ARTHUR'S SEX SECRETS

I **LIKE WOMEN.** *Let me clarify that. I like beautiful women. I know what you might say, "In the eyes of the beholder." That may be true. Everyone is different. I love beautiful women, the ones that turn your head walking down the street. The ones that turn you on, and "Johnny says Ooooooh."*

My beautiful woman has to be not overweight, not average, but slender and athletic. Not interested in average women. I want a woman who turns me on when I look at her. I want to immediately feel the desire to grab her and throw her on the kitchen table or sofa and make slow love to her. (Yes, I can still do it.) I want a woman who, when I wake up in the morning and I see her sleeping besides me, I think how lucky I am, and "Johnny" gets excited. I am her soulmate. I am part of her and she is part of me.

We think together. We know each other and we know what each other wants. Communication is important, as we know at all levels—we look at each other, and mentally send signals—I want you, NOW! We kiss passionately, with long, deep kisses whenever we can. We melt together.

A typical Saturday night. Cooking a meal together, having salmon that I caught in Alaska, along with peppers grilled with parmesan cheese (sneaking in a little hot pepper from my garden) and oregano for an appetizer. Maybe I will fry some zucchini or slice some fresh tomatoes (also from my garden) with mozzarella cheese, and basil from the garden. I do come from a farm in Kansas, and I do like to cook and love experimenting with flavors using herbs. Just like making love. They have a lot in common.

Anyway, let's get back to the dinner.

Dessert—I might make homemade ice cream and, depending on the season, I will garnish with currents, strawberries, blueberries, or raspberries from my garden. I might add a little triple sec, not too much, as homemade ice cream is delicate and delicious on its own.

By the way, when I make ice cream (the Kansas way), I make one gallon, in a hand crank freezer. You have to crank slow (just like in love-making) to get the cream to freeze on the inside of the container. It takes about thirty to forty minutes. Great time to talk and have a glass of wine or a cocktail. (By the way, why are drinks called "cocktail?")

When we made ice cream on the farm, we used to stop the turner in the raw milk tank, so the cream would rise to the top. Our ice cream was above 25% fat content. I was taught at the age of five how to make ice cream.

I am/was a spectroscopist, an analytical chemist, and a clinical chemist. I have a Masters in Chemistry, and an MBA "with distinction." I also had a chemistry scholarship while I was at Kansas State University. It paid me a whopping $100 a semester (which actually paid for my tuition.) I was also awarded a National Science Foundation Grant for doing research. Based upon my research, I published three papers. Not bad for a Kansas boy as an undergraduate. A wonderful evening with an old Bordeaux and listening to great music. I like classical—would you think a Kansas boy would like classical music?

After dessert, we would rinse the dishes (maybe let them sit for the next day if we got the urge to "cuddle")—I would come up behind her and hold her, moving against her body so she is between the sink and my body. I would move her hair to the left and I would kiss her lightly on her neck, nibbling on her ear. She would stop the water and enjoy the sensations flowing through her body. I use my hands to feel her body, starting at her shoulders, down to her waist, to her thighs, then to her buns. From there, I find my way slowly to her breasts. Her nipples would get hard as I softly and delicately squeeze her breasts. She would turn slowly, and kissing would begin.

I like breasts! They feel great. I just love them! My mother told me I loved to breast feed. Maybe that's the reason? It is also important that the woman likes the feel of hands on her breasts. Some don't—not interested in them. That's a shame for them.

After the dishes are rinsed, you can guess next. Both of us are sexually aroused.

To the bedroom, where we make love slowly. Soft music or a "romantic" movie to add to the evening. It might take an hour, but I believe it is important to satisfy the woman, maybe several times, before I do what is natural.

I have found that some women are not good lovers. I have found overweight women are the worst. Some other women are not too good either. Why, you ask? I can't answer for sure, but would assume either they were never taught, or not interested, or never fantasized. Maybe religion has something to do with it? Maybe their DNA? Maybe their hormones? Maybe their husbands were not good lovers? Maybe their mothers?

Women who take care of their bodies are the best lovers. They are not overweight and watch what they eat. They are active: running, skiing, kayaking, scuba, etc.

I was reading my notes in a dentist's office. A woman came and sat on my right. I know she was looking at my notes on what I was reading. I could sense that she was offended with the word SEX. Why are some women embarrassed with the word SEX? The woman, as soon as an empty chair was available, moved. I just grinned to myself. She wouldn't look at me as she got up to the dentist's examination room.

I wonder, down deep, if that woman was aroused or completely turned off. There are some women that sexually are not comfortable with men, even though they are married. (Why do you think the pool guy has a smile on his face?) I wonder if that may be the cause of divorce. Sex is powerful. The husband might want sex, and she doesn't want to have sex and is "cold."

Me? Once I start something, I want to finish. I want the woman to have the same pleasure of reaching orgasm as a man. At the age of seventy-six, I can't produce the amount of bodily fluid that I did as a twenty, thirty, forty, or a fifty-year-old.

The trick (for men) to making love is to have a woman that you are passionate about and would do anything for. You fantasize about her and what you want to do to her body.

People have been told that at fifty, sixty, or seventy, sex stops. Not true!

I have found that I am not the typical man at the age of seventy-six. I like sex! Lots of sex!

Let's go back.

I was born in Kansas in 1942. We had a farm but did not live there permanently. We lived in Topeka, Kansas. I worked on the farm during the summers with my uncle and aunt. I looked up to my uncle, as he was a gentle person and a person who could communicate with a twelve-year-old.

He taught me how to gather eggs. I hated that job. The damn hens would peck my hand when I tried to gather her eggs. True today with women? The peck hurt a little, but scared the shit out of me, because I knew I was going to get pecked as soon as my hand went under her.

To keep from getting any "serious injury," I used any way to get the hen out of the laying box. And I mean any way. I got the egg(s) and brought them into the house.

I was always asked, "Did you chase the hens out before you gathered the eggs?" The answer was always, "No!"

My uncle taught me how to drive a tractor at age twelve. I remember a time when I was sitting on my uncle's leg at age eleven and we were plowing a field for winter wheat. As we were plowing, we would disturb several rabbits' nests. The young rabbits and the adult rabbits would run down the furrow and field to escape. After plowing up several nests, my uncle stopped the tractor and told me to catch a little rabbit. I hopped off the tractor and ran after the small rabbit. Boy, can they run. I finally caught the rabbit after several tries.

One time, my uncle asked me if I wanted fried chicken or roast chicken. I said, "fried."

"Go out and get a rooster," he said.

There are several tricks to catching a rooster. I am not telling all my secrets! Within a few minutes, I had the rooster decapitated, let it bleed out, and brought it into the farm house.

He looked at the chicken and said, "I guess we are going to have roast chicken, because you killed a hen." I was twelve years old and felt stupid because I thought I knew the difference between a hen and a rooster.

On the farm I learned how to plow and disk the fields before planting wheat. I learned how to castrate a bull calf, milk a cow, shovel oats, wheats, etc., and help a heifer give birth.

What I am leading up to is that the farm life gave me experiences in many things, including sex. Most people never received the education I received. Every person should experience farm life.

Growing up in the Midwest, Scouting was big. At the age of thirteen, I had achieved the rank of Eagle Scout. I went on to get three palms: Bronze, Silver, and Gold. I traveled from Kansas to Illinois, and I walked for twenty-one miles in the footsteps of Abraham Lincoln to receive the Lincoln Trial Award. I went on to receive my "God and Country" award, and the "Silver Award"—the highest award in Exploring Scouting.

When I'd just finished my first year at Kansas State University, I had a job as a surveyor. I was surveying Interstate 80, which was close to the farm. So I came to the farm on weekends to help out. My uncle got me a date with a girl in the next town. As I was getting "spruced" up, my uncle came running in and asked me to help with a heifer giving birth. She was having a hard time—typical for a heifer. So I helped the mother-to-be. Needless to say, I was late for my date. No cell phone in those days. As a farm girl, my date understood my story.

Enough about my life. I just wanted to give some information about my childhood.

As a young man of seventy-six, and because of my upbringing of honest values, I do not think I am representative of the typical man in *his seventies. I have two simple rules, "Tell the truth and you don't have to remember what you say," and "My word is my bond." Maybe lawyers and politicians should follow these rules, as at law schools they teach* <u>*Lying 101.*</u>

I have found that men and women in our age bracket have many different opinions, experiences, many of them negative. These experiences have to be overcome to have an honest relationship.

Kissing is the best stimulation! There is something magical about lips when they touch. I knew the first time I kissed my ex-wife when I was in college that she was the ONE.

The chemistry (we were both chemists) was there. I knew it. We all know about when we kissed the person we loved.

Even today, I love to kiss. Kissing is as close to heaven as I can think of. Kissing stimulates my body and makes me want to use my hands.

I don't know the chemistry (even though I am a chemist) of what happens when you kiss. I just like the results. I have come to the conclusion that either you know how to kiss or you don't.

I have found that many women do not know how to kiss and are just bad kissers. The longer you kiss, from French-kissing to putting one's tongue between her teeth and gums, can be very sensuous. There are millions of nerve endings around the mouth and lips. Why not use them! If they get "Johnny" excited or "Sara" excited, why not do what our bodies are screaming for and help in the sexual satisfaction of our souls?

So, guys and gals, make sure you know how to kiss. If kissing doesn't turn you on, see me and I will help.

I believe in LOVE. Love is special. Love is different when you are in your seventies. You have been married. You may have kids. You may have grandkids. You have much experience under your belt. Use it to have fun!

Here are some questions I have been asked to answer:

A — What does the phrase "having sex" mean to you today? Is it different or similar to when you were thirty-five?

When I was thirty-five, I wanted, needed sex five days out of the week. Didn't always have it, as both my wife, kids, and I were busy.

First there were Elizabeth and Arthur. Elizabeth was seven years old and had already skipped kindergarten, so she was in 3rd grade. Arthur was three and in Montessori School. That was a busy time. Pick up kids, shopping, working, full-time. I was working on my career and doing a lot of traveling. When I was coming home on the plane, I would dream about making love to my wife when I got home. Fantasizing is great! I still fantasize.

Having sex or making love was when we could fit it in. What most men, me including, do not realize is how strong our wives are during those years. They become super-efficient. They are the best!

Now at seventy-six, with no kids, no wife, just work, it is not as tiresome as it was forty years ago.

So times were different. But the urge to have sex is still the same. Now it is more relaxed.

B — **How important is it for you to be in a sexual relationship now?**
VERY.

C — **What characteristics attract you today? Are they any different from when you were thirty-five?**

Same characteristics as thirty-five.

I, and I would assume a woman, would turn me on.

I have already stated my desires. I would guess every man is different. For example:

- *Some men like large breasts, some small. (I like a handful.)*
- *Some men like a big butt, some small. (I like a small butt.)*
- *Some men like a large woman. (Not me.)*
- *Some men like a slender woman. (That's me.)*
- *Some men like a smart woman. (That's me.)*
- *Some men like an athletic woman. (That's me.)*

The bottom line is you have to search until you find the perfect woman for you. Then sleep with her for a couple of years to really find out if you are compatible.

Remember, a lot of years have passed since you were in your twenties. You have become wise, set in your ways, have more money, etc. So has the opposite sex. It is difficult to find the right one.

D — Can a woman just charm you with her personality today? Do you need common interests today?

Not me. It helps though. Maybe the question should be chemistry instead of personality. Absolutely, you need common interests as you get older. Traveling has to be at the top of the list. Communication and feeling sexy together has to be even higher.

E — What turns you on today?

In terms of women, I assume? This has already been answered. A woman that makes you turn your head to look at her twice.

F — How aggressive do you want a woman to be? Do you want to be the seducer? What pleases you most today? Is it different from when you were younger?

I personally don't like aggressive women. To me that means argumentative, non-compromising. However, in terms of sex, that's different. It is important to try new things. A movie, a sex book, a magazine, a romantic movie.

There is nothing better than on a Sunday morning having a champagne breakfast in bed, watching a sexy, romantic movie. You relax and check out each other's bodies. You have to be eager to experiment. Any woman that says, "I don't like that" or says "No," is going to maybe create an unromantic relationship for some men. Some men like to be told what to do. I prefer a 50/50 decision, maybe 60/40.

It is important to be the seducer. With today's women on the "march," some women may want to be the seducer. I personally think I am going to get some shit that most women want to be seduced. I think we men want to be the seducer. Isn't it in our genes, or from the last thousand years that men were always larger in size? So they were in control.

However, a man is very easy to seduce. A beautiful woman, a woman who he is in love with. This man, however powerful, is like butter.

Take Cleopatra and Antony. She got her way to become one of the most powerful women in history. Actually, I think I would be like putty in her hands!

Kingdoms have been lost because of love. You can't stop it. The mind is a powerful part of our body. Once you get that "feeling" it's all over for both—especially for men.

G — Is it different from when you were younger?

Sex is sex. There is a pleasure that can't be described. The first time I had sex, that was the greatest sensation I have ever felt. I said to myself, I would love to feel like that all the time.

I am of the few people in the world who has never taken any drugs, including marijuana. Never tried it, never wanted to, but I am guessing that drugs provide a similar feeling. Though for me, nothing wrong with the good bottle of wine or a dirty martini.

H — Do you feel like old wine? Just as you get older, are you sexually more astute? Better? Enjoy it more or less?

This is not a fair question to me. I have a Bordeaux collection. When it comes to red wine, I especially like fifteen to twenty-year-old Bordeaux wine. Don't like cheap or young wines. I have made wine, and the older the wine, the smoother it is. That's the way I like my women.

Getting older has nothing to do with sex. It has more to do with your companion when you look at her, do you get the urge to grab her. If the answer is no, then you have a bad sex life.

I — What pleases me most?

A billion dollars would help. Knowing I am going to live to 100 and be active. A wonderful woman by my side that still turns me on, etc.

If you are still talking about sex—keeping Johnny excited or just thinking about a woman at my age, wondering if Johnny is going to keep on producing.

J — Do you have any advice for older women, or older men, to enjoy themselves more, or for older men to enjoy themselves more, or enhance their attractiveness more?

Sure. Exercise! It stimulates the chemical endorphins and increases our serotonin. Whenever I exercise, ski, whitewater raft, kayak, or split firewood, etc., I get horny! Nothing better than cuddling, having good wine in front of a fireplace after skiing.

Slim down. I find men and women, the older they get, they put on weight in all the wrong places.

When you were in college, the prettiest girls and boys were slim. They have been athletic. If you feel good, look good, then you will be good.

K — Do you believe in one sexual partner at a time, now?

If you are married, yes.

L — Do you see yourself at any point just "forgetting" about a sexual relationship because it's too much work, or too much stress, or just annoying to have someone else in your life?

You're kidding me—absolutely not!

The best sex is spontaneous sex. Don't plan on it. When you get the urge, elevators are good; in the woods; in the shower (great, but getting harder to do); used to love to do it in the car, but now cars are not convenient. Someplace spontaneous, and be spontaneous.

In college, a blanket was always in the trunk. There is nothing better than making love with someone that you are truly in love with.

I say to all,

HAVE A GREAT LIFE AND MAKE LOVE

CHAPTER FIVE

MORTALITY AND OTHER DISCOMFORTS

ERE I AM, SITTING AT MY KITCHEN TABLE AT 6:30 in the morning, sipping coffee and skimming my Wall Street Journal. I turn to the Health Care section and I see, jumping out at me, a large colored picture of a birthday cake absolutely loaded with candles. Next to the picture is written in large bold letters, **"Is There a Limit To the Human Lifespan?"** (*Wall Street Journal*, June 25, 2018. B1.)

Wow, I thought, what could be a better lead-in for this chapter on our mortality in a book about senior dating and mating than an article on how long we might expect to live?

THINKING ABOUT MORTALITY IS A
VERY HUMAN CONDITION

Only the human being has the capacity to think about lifespan, aging, quality of life, and death.

To this day, naturalists have failed to find any hint that animals think into the future, worry about their life, think about their quality of life, wonder whether or not they will have a long life, or wonder how, when, or where they will die. Animals live from day to day. Animals forage. Animals procreate. Animals defend their territories. Their thought processes are limited to their immediate concerns. What few thoughts animals may have about their future, we call "animal instinct."

The one animal that is an exception is the homo-sapiens, the human being—you and me.

In this vast animal kingdom, to which we belong, we are the only animals who think about mortality. We think about our lives; the quality of our lives; whether or not we will be long-lived; and how, when, and where we will die.

We think about our future. We plan for our future. We speculate about our future. We worry about our future. We think about the future of people around us. We worry about our environment because we worry if it will be there to sustain us. We worry about our planet on which we live. We believe in a god, because we fear the future. We talk about mortality. We talk about our health. We write articles on our mortality. We write about our expectations of our death. We write articles on extending our lifespan. We publish articles in mass-distributed newspapers questioning and analyzing our lifespan.

For us human beings, our lifespan—our mortality—is a deadly serious matter.

WHEN DOES DYING BEGIN?

Thinking and dealing with our mortality is a discomforting thought. Discomfort may not sound like the right word, but it is the right word. By the age of sixty, we are never totally free of our thoughts of our health—when our end might come—when our life might be over.

As we hit our sixties, all of us have begun to face the facts of aging. Our eyesight is dimmer. Our hearing is more impaired. We notice we are moving slower. Jokingly, we say the stairs are steeper, the newsprint is smaller, the streets are longer.

We are talking about our place in the workplace. We start talking about retirement. Our government is telling us we are getting old. Government help is beginning to kick in. We start thinking about when to stop contributing to our IRAs, and start withdrawing. We start receiving robo-calls advising us we need a medical alert system.

We are looking at the assets we have accumulated. We are wondering how we are going to live for the next ten to thirty years. We are worried that while our ability to maintain our earnings is becoming more limited, we are also increasing our lifespans. According to statistics, we are maintaining our health longer, which, of course, feeds into our increased longevity.

But we must not let our fears and concerns overwhelm us. Particularly, as senior citizens, our aging and our mortality are concerns we *must* compartmentalize. As uncomfortable as it may be, our thoughts about our dying are concerns we have to endure, accept, or fight against—as our personality dictates. We need to "live till we die." The closer we get, agewise, to what we consider "old age," the harder we must work to compartmentalize.

So that's why we need to talk about our mortality in a book about our dating and mating starting in our sixties. We know our mortality is closer to us than ever before. We are more worried about it than ever before. We are more worried about it as we meet new people with whom we might want to establish a relationship. We are worried not only about our mortality, but the possible lifespan of the person we have just met.

Here's one way to think about your mortality versus dating and meeting someone in your sixty-plus years. Think of whether to date and mate as you enter your seventies, eighties, and nineties in terms of a cost-benefit decision. Here is the question: What does entrance into the singles world, "putting yourself out there in the social world" in the last trimester of your life, cost *versus* the loneliness, the solitude, the emptiness you might feel by going it alone?

Each of us will have our own individual answer.

WHEN DO WE ENTER OUR OLD AGE?

Remember Pearl? You met her in Chapter 2, "Busy, Busy, Busy." Pearl wanted to start dating again at seventy-six years old. Remember she said, "I am a young person trapped in an old person's body." It was in the 1980s when Pearl made that statement. If she were seventy-six today, in 2018, she might not have said her body was "old."

Remember the day when you learned how your parents felt about their aging? Your mom probably confessed to you when she turned forty, she knew she was getting old. Remember when your dad said that turning forty he felt he was over the hill? Remember, when your parents talked about their retirement, they would say, why save for retirement...most of us are not going to get there. Retirement was the age of sixty-five. Period. A man's life expectancy was in his sixties. A woman's life expectancy was somewhere in her seventies. Our parents, as they began to feel old(er) at forty, could not envision a second life, a renewal, or a "second wind."

When we thought that forty years old was entering early old age, we worried about cancer, diabetes, heart attacks, muscular problems, arthritis, Parkinson's disease. We worried whether we had put away enough money to help our kids through their formative ages. Our parents took out lots of insurance. We got married earlier.

So what we think about when we are seventy, our parents thought about when they turned forty. The worries were there, perhaps in a different combination, but worries about mortality, disease, longevity, health, and happiness were and continue to be simply a part of mankind's understanding that we do not have the ability to live forever.

Our fears and concerns about our mortality remain the same, no matter what age we start to think about it. Today, these fears, these worries, these fatalisms start later. The emphasis may have changed somewhat, as the medical profession and scientists find drugs to combat, slow down, or manage our physical breakdowns. We have cholesterol-lowering drugs, drugs to control our sugar, drugs to keep our blood pressure in check. We are finding drugs to combat the onslaught of Alzheimer's disease. We fear prostate cancer and breast cancer, but less, because of advances in medical science.

Not that long ago, Alzheimer's disease was combined with other forms of cognitive impairment under the general umbrella term "dementia." Dementia was an expected symptom of old age. Today, Alzheimer's has been defined by itself as a disease. The fear of getting the disease named after Dr. Alois Alzheimer is in the mind of every aging man and woman.

Gerontologists and geriatric doctors are marveling over the slowing down of the aging process, thanks in part to modern medical science, nutrition, and mass communication, i.e., the sharing of information amongst the lay population. So, although we are living longer, we do not hide or minimize our health issues as we did ten years or so ago.

Even though we are older, our dating and mating experiences more closely resemble folks in their thirties, forties, and fifties—more than ever before. There are adjustments, as we shall see. The sense of mortality is much more upon us, and we all need to deal with it.

In today's world of older folk, we continue to think about our aging, but we believe we can slow down the aging process. We can manage our aging.

WHAT SHOULD WE BE CALLED?

I have been wondering—trying to figure out, if you will—what to call the general population of sixty-five-year-olds and over. Now is a good time to bring the subject up. Are we "seniors?" Seniors is the word I have been using throughout this book. I find it comfortable. We all remember our school days. I believe the word gives us dignity. Maybe an edge over others, those other folk who are younger than we are. *Say, 59?* While "younger" is a word that may connote beauty and vigor, which we all would like, to me, "seniors" connotes seniority—power over others. I like to think that being a senior puts me above those younger than I, even though their skin is less wrinkled and their walk is faster. In this day of equality, where we are exhorted to feel and act equal to our brethren, no matter what, there is still that smidgen of feeling above and below according to age. Or at least I am hoping that there is still that smidgen of feeling. "Open the door for me, you whippersnappers, 'I'm your senior.' Give me the respect I am due, just for my being your senior," we should be thinking as we trudge our ways through our daily activities.

I have read articles on this. Just recently I read a signed article (a five-column article, no less, labeled *Turning Points)* in a national newspaper headlined, "Forget 'SENIOR' – Boomers Search for a Better Term." Boomers refers to that bumper crop of kids born in the late 1940s-50s because of the end of World War II. It is mostly a negative article about the use of words "seniors," "elderly," "aging," or "aged." The author states the boomers are purportedly suggesting society use different words to replace the word "senior" for the population over sixty-five years old. Boomers are unhappy about the label "seniors" because "the word sounds like it comes out of civics class" and "there are a whole bunch of older people who are nothing close to wise." The author states that the only word some boomers have come up with to replace "seniors" is the word *"Perennial."*

Do you, dear reader, want to be referred to as a *Perennial?*

Whether or not modern society (including our own boomers who are entering our beloved class of seniorhood) challenges our rightful place as being the head of the class or the smartest, brightest, and the future of the school, I write this to repeat we can have both respect for our senior age, and the freedom to have a wonderful seniorhood. My vote is for "seniors."

MEN RESPOND TO MY QUESTIONS
ABOUT THEIR MORTALITY

When I asked single senior males the open-ended question, how do they envision their death, the great majority of the men stated, "I want to go the way Rockefeller went." Nelson Rockefeller, to whom they are referring, was Governor of New York in the 1960s and was Vice President of the United States in the 1970s. He died suddenly of a heart attack when he was seventy years old. Where he died was on the minds of the men I spoke to. Rockefeller, as it turned out, was caught with his "pants down"; that is, he died of a heart attack when he was with a woman who was his secretary—*not* his wife.

"That's the way I want to go," to paraphrase the men I interviewed.

I found the answer funny, in a way. Rockefeller was seventy years old, and I am asking this question of men who are over seventy and have outlived Rockefeller. They were not taken aback when I pointed the discrepancy out. Stubbornly, they refused to treat my comment as an either/or question. They responded by holding their ground, stating they still wanted to go like Rockefeller, only later.

In all fairness, looking back at 1979 when Rockefeller died, male longevity was somewhere from the late sixties to the middle seventies. So when the event happened, Nelson Rockefeller was considered by society to die at the natural age for old men.

It seems, if I read my male interviewees right, they want to die having a good time. Men accept their mortality and ask only that they have a good time until the day they die. And for them, what could be better than getting laid?

Women responded in a totally different way.

If the men see themselves leaving our world with a "bang," then women see themselves leaving our world with a "whimper."

WOMEN RESPOND TO MY QUESTIONS
ABOUT THEIR MORTALITY

When I asked single senior females the open-ended question, how do they envision their death, the great majority of the women responded in terms of a "slowing down." They said they saw themselves becoming more infirm. All they said they hoped for was to live to a ripe old age. Just hoped they would not be a burden to others. Their concerns were much more fear of contracting Alzheimer's, breast or other cancers, or other diseases than of living until the day they died. They believed if they were able to take care of themselves properly, they could live longer. Having fun was not a part of their equation. Their death would creep up, come upon them slowly. They do not mind breaking down, being able to only live life in a more limited way. They could adjust to their aging. They just wanted to continue to live and be a part of the world in whatever manner they could.

AGE IS JUST A NUMBER—OR IS IT?

Gerontologists (those folks who study aging) have divided the term OLD AGE into three subdivisions: Early Old Age ("EOA")—our seventies; Middle Old Age ("MOA") – our eighties; and Old Old Age ("OOA")—our nineties.

That's okay—for starters. But our bodies do age at different rates, a factor not considered by labels provided by the gerontologists. We see that fact most clearly as we enter into our seventies, eighties, and nineties. As we enter our senior years, we become aware of a growing disparity between the health, conduct, and looks among folks within the same age group.

Here are a few examples of where the chronological age of the senior fails to describe the senior's total persona in his/her relationship to other seniors.

— Patrick and Harold —

Both Patrick and Harold are gentlemen in their mid-seventies. Patrick shuffles when he walks. He has had a few stents put into his heart over the past few years. He is on a number of drugs, including a blood pressure drug and a statin for his heart problems, which he claims slows him down.

Patrick's social preferences include movies, restaurants, and conversations. He belongs to a book club, and goes to the Y for lectures and conversations. Harold has a more active lifestyle. He prefers going to the gym on a bi-weekly basis. He is taking a carpentry class at the Y. Harold's social preferences include walks and traveling. He plays Pickleball at least once a week, and says he feels great after it.

— Jim and John —

Jim is eighty-two, in visually good shape: fairly trim, small bellied, and quite muscular. John is seventy-two, also in visually good shape: fairly trim, small bellied, and quite muscular. Ten years' difference in age. But both appear to be the same age.

Both men are still working. Both men run small companies. Jim is in the printing business. John is in the perfume fragrance manufacturing business.

Yet Jim walks with a fast, spritely gait, walks up and down stairs easily, and walks rather long distances without stopping. John, the younger man by almost ten years, shuffles as he walks, has trouble going up and down stairs, and needs to rest when walking more than two blocks. John has had medical problems since his thirties. He admits to the acceleration of his problems after sixty.

Their leisure activities show the state of their health.

Jim at eighty-two still skis with a senior citizen ski club. Jim at eighty-two takes off with the "boys" for an annual fly-fishing expedition for salmon in Alaska. When Jim travels, he prefers travels that provide some exercise—those that might involve hiking and walking. Jim, by the way, is self-deprecating in reporting his activities. He states, with a sheepish and sad expression on his face, that he no longer even thinks of a bicycle trip, or a safari type of trip. Jim claims to be a mere shadow of himself.

John, ten years younger than Jim at seventy-two, has given up tennis "a long time ago." He plays a few rounds of golf. Golf is his only sport. He prefers to sit at the TV and immerses himself in sports programs most weekends. He does not go out to eat in restaurants because he finds lots of foods disagree with him. He visits his grown son who lives in the next town as often as he is invited. He finds this kind of activity relaxing and bonding. He looks forward to any socializing he can do, as long as it is not too arduous.

Both men have visited dating sites. Both men have met women and dated women from these dating sites.

— Louise and Anne —

Louise is eighty-two, in visually good shape: quite trim, well-turned out, feminine in her appearance. Anne is seventy-two, also in visually good shape. Quite trim, well-turned out, feminine in her appearance. Side by side, it would be difficult if not impossible to guess their ages, and to even guess who was the elder.

Both women are still working. Louise is a residential real estate broker in the fast-paced world of New York condos, co-ops and townhouses. She claims her business keeps her on her toes. Anne is a lawyer, a sole practitioner, working out of her apartment. She claims she works around the clock. She complains she has too many clients, she makes herself too available for their complaints. She goes to court once in a while, and meets with clients once in a while in a downtown office, where she rents a conference room from time to time.

Louise walks with a fast, rapid gait for "a woman of her age." She uses public transportation as much as possible. She handles stairs okay and has stamina for a bunch of city blocks. Louise is constantly pushing herself to keep physically active. She claims to love the exercise associated with her "earning a living."

Anne is much more sedentary than Louise. She bemoans the fact that she does not feel comfortable in heels any more, and she takes as many physical shortcuts as her budget will allow.

Louise has taken yoga. Now she enjoys dance classes. When she travels, she looks for the adventure part of it. Nothing too sedentary. She doesn't want to be chaperoned around a city on an excursion bus.

Anne, on the other hand, watches lots of television, and communicates with her extensive group of girlfriends by phone and email. She doesn't feel comfortable with a man who professes he is athletic because she does not want to "keep up." Or, as she said, at least she does not want to feel she is being left behind.

So, if you are a physically active man who would want to have your woman with you on your long walks, hikes, fishing trips, or as a golf companion, whose companionship would you prefer, Anne or Louise? Who would you rather have sex with?

So, if you are a thoughtful, contemplative woman, would you rather continue dating John or Jim?

I am not looking to hear your answer, obviously. The reason why I introduced these single seniors to you now is to really raise the issue of just how important chronological age is or should be in your dating and mating choices. There is no absolute answer. Only your decision.

THE "ANTI-AGING" MOVEMENT AND PROCESS

Today, mortality is no longer considered a fatalism, expected and acknowledged. If we put up with the discomfort of worry about it, talking about it, networking about it, anxiety about it, we have the ability to slow it down. Our continuing discourse over our aging process makes us less fatalistic about our mortality. Now we are told we can fight the disease, or slow down its Progress. If we pay attention—with treatment by others and by self-treatment—we can prevent it.

Anti-aging is not something your parents would have talked about. They did not think in those terms. All they hoped for was to have science and medicine stop enough of the progression of their diseases to die more comfortably. They were skeptical of the "cure rate." "Remission" was not expected. The most they could hope for was some form of "management." Diseases like Parkinson's or diabetes were diseases to be suffered.

Our parents' goal was to die of natural causes. Natural causes meant their bodies were breaking down, naturally. They hoped to die in their sleep. Death was immutable. Just needed to make it more comfortable. When their number was up…their number was up.

Now: *Parkinson's disease?* It can be controlled and managed. *Cancer?* It can be put into remission. *Diabetes?* It can be managed. *Alzheimer's?* Any day now, there will be a cure.

We are living in a world of "anti-aging."

In today's world of older folk, we are still thinking about our aging, but we believe we can slow down the aging process. We can manage our aging. For the more positive thinkers among us, we can get our "second wind." We can "live until we die."

The word "anti-aging" first entered into the American vocabulary in the 1940s when skin cream companies used the expression to sell their face and hand creams.

Around 1991, "anti-aging" entered into American society's mindset as a process to turn back the clock—to slow down the body's aging process. Anti-aging was no longer just a word or phrase to describe a particular product. It became a movement where groups of people from all walks of life began working for a common goal to retard our aging and to set back our biological clock. Based originally on medical science—mostly chemistry and biology—to prevent the aging process, it now encompasses many disciplines, many types of practitioners, many types of research, and common folks like you and me.

The anti-aging movement has an academy called "American Academy of Anti-Aging Medicine." Called "A4M" for short, the Academy was founded in 1993 by two American osteopaths. The goal of the Academy is stated as "the advancement of technology to detect, prevent, and treat aging-related disease and to promote research into methods to retard and optimize the human aging process." More simply, co-founder and president Ronald Klatz was quoted as stating, "We're not about growing old gracefully. We're about never growing old."

The A4M is now located in 110 countries, and boasts over 26,000 physicians and practitioners, researchers, health providers, and concerned members of the public. A World Congress is held annually.

Even though the field of anti-aging is still not recognized as a legitimate scientific movement by medical organizations such as the American Medical

Association, the field of anti-aging has entered into the mainstream of American life, and in the life of societies around the globe.

Unfortunately, today, even where so many older (and even younger) folk ingest vitamins and supplements as prevention of aging, their benefits are not acknowledged by the medical profession or our government. That is because, to this day, the anti-aging world as a real benefit to our lives, to forestall our aging process, continues to be fractured among different commercial groups. There is the pharmaceutical industry and the "supplement" industry. Most doctors do not recommend any supplements. Why? Because the FDA does not test them. Why doesn't the FDA test them? Because the pharmaceutical industry has spent money for research and development for their drugs and needs to be reimbursed by the consumer/patient.

Another example of the "fractured" anti-aging movement is the division between rehabilitation and the problem to be cured. In India, if a person has a knee problem, her post-operation rehabilitation therapist may very well be in the operating room, and observing the operation herself or himself. The therapist is under the responsibility of the operating doctor, and she/he will be answering to the doctor. After the operation, the patient begins to undergo physical therapy. The physical therapist must report the progress to the doctor. The doctor has the ultimate responsibility. Compare this treatment to U.S. treatment. The doctor writes a prescription; you probably have a choice of therapists; the prescription has maybe two words on it, and off you go. There is no automatic follow-up. There is really no accountability. There is really no post-operative rehabilitation concern. Here, medical science says the operation is a success and off you go. Do not come back unless there is a problem. In other societies, as you just learned, as in India, the success of the operation is continued into the patient's after-operation life. There is a continuum of care utilizing more than one specialty.

Anti-aging is a process as well as a movement. Fighting the aging of our bodies (physically and mentally) requires the interaction of different disciplines, skills, and products for the health, well-being, and longevity of the individual. The process involves people from all walks of life, all backgrounds, all levels of educational achievement. It involves scientists, doctors of medicine, psychologists, engineers, therapists, cosmetologists, nutritionists, you and me.

Today, the anti-aging process is the central mission of some medical professionals, i.e., Doctors of Medicine and Doctors of Osteopathy. Often, they call their practices, "Wellness Centers." Within their practice, they often refer to those who come to them as clients, not patients. They practice what is called "alternative," "complementary" or "integrative" medicine.

Today, the anti-aging process includes new drugs. Not drugs so much to fight a medical problem like antibiotics against infections, or vaccines against diseases like the measles, or blood pressure-lowering drugs. But drugs that alter our biological and chemical makeup to bring us back to a healthier (younger?) state. These "new" drugs are new because they are designed to replace our body hormones that we produce less of as we age. Estrogen replacement medications and testosterone replacement medications are in this category. Replacement of stem cells, a young and new field of scientific investigation, promises to repair and replace our "lost" health and "lost" prowess.

Today, the anti-aging process includes non-medical physical therapists. These people are personal trainers, yoga instructors, Pilates instructors, and others. They promise to bring us back to a physically viable state, or to slow down our physical degeneration. We go to fitness classes, fitness gyms, or buy DVDs of exercise programs tailored to our senior needs and play them on our own DVR, at our own speed, on our own time. We will remain stronger, more flexible, with more stamina, as we live onward into our nineties.

Today, the anti-aging process includes nutritionists who are giving us advice on eating healthy. Our TVs are full of programs on eating healthy. Our TVs are full of programs on weight control.

Today, the anti-aging treatment includes consumption of vitamin pills and supplements to replenish our bodies' needs when our bodies begin to fail to produce them on their own. Vitamins, supplements, natural enhancements, and "healthy diets" have slowly but surely entered into the American mindset.

Not one of my 100 or so interviewees told me they took "nothing." At the very least, they took a one-a-day vitamin.

Today, the anti-aging process includes machinery constructed by engineers and scientists and doctors working together to create devices that massage you, cool your body, or heat your body: cryonics therapy for rejuvenation and cures. Pulsed electromagnetic or pulsed radio therapy for our damaged tissues and muscles. Machines using light (available for home purchase) to apply to our skin and stimulate it to create collagen.

Then there is you and me. We are part of the anti-aging process because we are telling each other around the dinner table what's new, what we recommend, and what we are trying. We are honest with each other. We admit to cosmetic procedures, because we know if we think we look better, we feel better. Do not discount the importance of your role in the anti-aging process of all of us.

We have learned, or are at least told, that if we fight our disease, if we energize against it, we may be able to beat it. Remember John Wayne? John Wayne, our all-American cowboy-hero. Remember that he was stricken with cancer? All of us would read and hear how John Wayne was fighting his cancer. We never learned what exactly was going on but we sure imagined John Wayne pulling out his pistol and taking aim at his enemy—his cancer.

Our parents would have laughed at that image. But then again, our parents never heard of "free radicals" or "antioxidants" either.

We have learned, or are at least told, that if we look better, we will feel better. If we feel better, we will have more energy to fight our free radicals invading our body, out to kill us. We can all be John Wayne in our personal battle against our aging.

We are no longer considered vain when we engage in treatments that seem only to affect our physical demeanor. Men and women today use dermatological products to tighten their sagging arms, their creeping thighs, wrinkles, and crow's lines from their faces. Hair loss is no longer inevitable. There are products to stop it. Botox injections for wrinkles are now being advertised to men.

One of the busiest and most well-known plastic surgeons in the New York area remarked to me that plastic surgery is growing for all women, in all age groups. Also, more men are coming to him for facelifts. He has performed cosmetic procedures on folks well into their eighties because they are demanding it. He performs the surgery in nine out of ten requests because he finds they are healthy enough to undergo surgery. He claimed to have performed a facelift on someone as old as ninety-one years old—successfully.

Also, he sees a much wider spectrum of male and female enhancements, including fillers, laser treatments, breast implants, liposuction, way up into their eighties.

We all know or have heard of someone who still skis in his/her eighties. Years ago, there were so few folks over seventy who skied that the ski slopes would offer free or almost free ski lift tickets to the seniors. The ski resort figured they would get the seniors to the slope and would at least be able to generate extra food income. But so many post-seventy-year-olds would now show up that the ski slopes have either raised their age barrier to seventy-five and eighty, or have just stopped doing it altogether.

As you read earlier, gerontologists have divided the term OLD AGE into three subdivisions: "EOA"—our seventies; "MOA"—our eighties; and "OOA"—our nineties.

Gerontologists are giving credit for the slowing down of the aging process and for increasing longevity to advances in medical science. But they have begun to acknowledge, also, the importance of non-medicine areas such as nutrition, physical activity, and a person's psychological mindset as connected to a person's living a longer and healthier, more energetic life.

Perhaps, in a generation or so, we will be able to extend the chronological timing of these designations. According to the life extension and anti-aging experts, there is no reason why the human cannot live well into his/her 100s. They point out the oldest living human has been verifiably clocked in as dying at 122 years old.

CAN WE RESET OUR SEXUAL CLOCKS?

Our Senior Years Can be Golden Years for Older Folks' Sexuality.

As you read in Chapter 3, there has been a sexual revolution among the older folks. We have come to understand we are sexual beings until the day we die. Seniors over sixty continue to have a need and an interest to follow up on their inherent sexual needs by dating and mating.

Today, we have choices in our march toward our mortality. Our choices depend upon our mindset. Our mindset also determines our sexual conduct. Even intercourse, meaning sexual penetration, has become a matter of choice.

We acknowledge that "older men," which we are using for seventy-year-olds, take longer to have an erection. Their erections are less firm and are shorter-lived compared to when they were in their twenties. At the age of thirty, men begin to produce less testosterone. After sex, it takes longer for men to become re-aroused. Male menopause, called andropause, ranges mostly in the fifties.

But now, we understand we have some options in dealing with it. Now, as seventy, eighty, and ninety-year-olds, we are offered options to extend our sexual life. Men are using a penis ring, vacuum device, injection, pellet therapy, ESWT (electro-shock wave therapy), and other treatments to increase or maintain their ability to have intercourse and to ejaculate.

We talked about Bob Dole in Chapter 3, "Sex and the Single Senior." Remember?

Remember, he was seventy-five years old—well into his "early old-age" (using the gerontologists' label) when he told the nation that Viagra made him a sexual man again.

For the first time, it was publicly advanced by a real, trustworthy person that given the proper treatment, a dysfunctional part will be transformed into *function*.

Our parents had to take it or leave it. Had to take whatever happened. Whatever your dad may have taken to preserve his sexuality was outside the realm of medical acceptance. By and large, our parents took your dad's impotence as part of getting old—meaning after forty! We do not even use the word "impotence" any longer. We call it "erectile dysfunction." Using the term (shortened now to **ED**) gives it the connotation that it is curable. Way back then, in those seemingly ancient days of 1998, when a man could not get an erection, he was called impotent. Doesn't impotence sound like a permanent state? In 1998, the general consensus was that when a man became impotent, he was finished sexually.

We have the ability to keep our sexual libido going, to act out in our sexual life, until the day we die. Think of it this way. Where we take our blood pressure pill to keep our blood pressure down to the day we die...we could also be taking our estrogen replacement therapy to keep our vaginas moist, or Viagra to create an erection.

Science and medicine now tells us we must use it or lose it. Science and medicine are now telling us that sex is healthy for the body. We must treat intercourse like a muscular exercise.

Also, as a reminder, we are defining the sexual side of our being, as an indescribable, almost symptomless need to be in a sexual relationship. This relationship is not based on any overt characteristics. It defies description. It is just as Justice Potter Stewart described pornography, saying in effect, I cannot describe porn, but **"I know it when I see it."**

We cannot describe (yet) what we mean by sexual attraction, but we know it when it happens. Today, we are told that our sexual attraction and our sexual attractiveness can remain with us until the day we die.

The men I spoke to exhibited variety in their responses to their sexual decisions. All the men I have spoken to, well almost all, say "I am not what I used to be." They are also referring to muscular slowdowns. "I can't run/jog the way I used to. I used to be able to mow the lawn. I could lift those suitcases. I was able to help my wife out. Now I don't even feel like taking out the garbage." But when it came to intercourse and ejaculation, their responses ranged from a determination to "get it up, and get laid" to the feeling of sexual attraction was all they needed to make a relationship work.

The women also exhibited variety in their responses. Many of the women stated they felt sexually freer in their sixties-plus. They no longer had to worry about getting pregnant. They no longer had to worry about their privacy. Most of them were living alone. Or, if in an assisted living facility, had their own rooms. Many, not all of course, expressed a need and a desire to enjoy sex more than they did when younger, when hampered by their own bodies and circumstances. As dating and mating women, many elected to take hormonal therapy or supplements to enhance their libido. Others, like some men I interviewed, simply said they did not need intercourse or want intercourse. They just knew a relationship was happening when it happened.

Even though we are older, our dating and mating experiences more closely resemble folks in their thirties, forties, and fifties than ever before. There are differences, of course. When younger folks have health setbacks, they treat them more like "bad luck"—something they will overcome. When we have health setbacks starting in our sixties, we treat them like forerunners of our mortality. "Is this the beginning of the end?" we ask. We all need to deal with our sense of our impending mortality. Some of us work hard to increase our libido, regardless of whether we can get it up, or create the environment to let it in.

You will see from the following stories how some of us deal with it.

— Gary —

Gary is eighty-seven years old. He is strong-looking. His voice is deep and strong. When seated, he gives the impression of virility and focus. However, he can barely walk. His "legs feel very heavy." His body is stiff.

I asked him what he thinks about his age. His response was, "I don't think much about it anymore. To me, age is a number, a chronological number. If I were to respond immediately that I am pushing ninety, I would say I would be mortally afraid. But somehow, and I don't know when it happened, I think of age as how vital I feel."

When I asked him about his social life, he responded, "I get around. Have a 'lady friend' and we have dinner together twice a week, go to the theater together. She's in about the same shape as I am, but we manage."

He took Viagra for about ten years, but has since given it up. No longer so important to "get it up" anymore.

When I told him the Rockefeller story, he said, "Ah yes, I remember it well. But that was 'then,' and 'now is now.' For me, now, intellectual companionship is sexy."

— Walter —

Walter is a widower in his seventies. He has neuropathy of his feet. He has a disability permit for his car. When I first met him, he had been widowed for about seven months. He said that he went through a period of severe depression after the loss of his wife. She had been his soulmate. They were "two peas in a pod."

But he went online to meet someone. "Why?" I asked. He answered, "Because I saw how desperately I needed a body alongside me in bed." He went on to say that he was unable to have an erection, and therefore unable to have intercourse. But he would be as happy just to have a woman beside him. Of course, it would have to be a woman with whom he felt that chemical attraction. Not every woman, of course. "I am not Charlie Harper in *Two and a Half Men*."

He went on to say that he was confident that he would attract a woman who was similar to him...and that he would find her sexually compatible. Meaning she herself would not need internal penetration to be a sexual and full partner.

His goal was re-marriage.

I understand now that he has a girlfriend of six months, and they are considering moving in together.

— **Dennis** —

Do you remember the word "spry"? It was a word my parents used for a man in his eighties or so who seemed agile, nimble, energetic, vigorous, animated, full of life "for a man of his age."

I have not heard that word used in years. But that's the word that came to my mind when I interviewed Dennis.

At eighty-nine years old, Dennis looked every bit his age. But his persona was that of true vigor. He spoke with enthusiasm. He almost jumped up from his chair as he offered to refill my drink. He became a widower at seventy-five years old. He's had two girlfriends since then. His last girlfriend had passed away a few months before I was introduced to him.

How do I handle my impending mortality, you ask?

I can't say I handle it at all. I just go on living. I have a routine every day. I go to my local gym. I have a personal trainer there, once a week. The other times, I just go it alone. I love looking at the girls on the machines. It gives me a boost. I've made friends there. Everyone knows me. I correct that. Most everyone knows me. I've had the same personal trainer for the past few years. They seem to come and go. I seem to outlast my personal trainers. No, I do not call them physical therapists. They are not physical therapists. What's the point of thinking of our physical well-being as a medical problem? It's not a medical problem, but a lifestyle choice. Yes, I know that Medicare pays for physical therapy, but I don't care. I make that choice because it makes me feel younger. I am hanging out with the younger folk.

I've had things done. You see my teeth? They are all capped. Now I have a bright smile. I actually capped them when I was sixty-four. That was well before all the smile improvement places became popular. I've had hair transplants. I started having them when I was in my fifties. After sixty-eight, it was enough.

I had a really good time in my marriage. We tried to overcome the problems and stresses of raising our family and tried to laugh a lot.

Don't believe that bullshit that after a long marriage, the man kind of falls apart when his wife dies. At least, it wasn't true about me. Yes, she took care of me. I never went into the kitchen. That kind of thing. But after she passed, I went to cooking school at the Y. Let me tell you, it was a lot of fun. And I started dating again.

I never went on a dating site. Didn't have to. There are wonderful single gals all around me.

My sexual appetite took a nosedive in my later years. My wife and I did not have sex for at least six or seven years before she passed. Life was comfortable. But sex was gone. After she passed, though, I started fantasizing again. Most of the time it was with Brigitte Bardot. Although I did switch to Catherine Deneuve once in a while. Aren't they every man's fantasy? Sometime or other in a man's life?

At my urologist check-up, I asked about sexual enhancements so I can get my buddy working again. I've been going to the same urologist for at least ten years—to watch my prostate –you know. I went on Cialis, then Viagra. I had penile injections. My erections came back. I think they simply jump-started me. Like, you know, jump-starting a car. (He grinned as he said this.) But I don't think it was the drugs that have kept me going. I think my libido is back. I feel renewed sexually by all you sexy gals out there.

No, I do not chase younger women. I do love to look at them though. But when it comes to love, to an actual relationship, I am more comfortable, more attracted to women within my age group...give or take ten years.

I really don't want to know my woman's age. I never ask, for sure. If I want her, I want her. The ball is in her court whether or not she's going to go to bed with me.

I have not always been a picture of health, you know. I had a stroke—very minor stroke—as it turned out when I was sixty-four years old. But it left its mark on me psychologically.

Life is precious. Enjoy it. Take it as it comes. Deal with it. Don't let your problems stop you from living it until you die.

— Rose —

Rose is a slim, petite seventy-seven-year-old. She's had two hip replacements, but still has trouble walking. She always uses a foldable cane when on the street, but closes it and puts it away when she comes inside.

Rose said she is up front with her dates, telling them she does not engage in intercourse. She said she tries to put it as tactfully as possible, but she wants to get that out of the way as soon as possible so there is no misunderstanding or discomfort. She is also up front whether she wants to see the man again.

Rose informed me that she is too dry inside and does not want to insert "any of that crap" into her vagina. Although she is sweet and feminine-looking, her face is quite lined, and her hair is stark white. She stated that she doubted whether she could still spread her legs enough to allow penetration.

Then she stated, with a wide grin, she is dating. And she is meeting men who also are not interested in penetration—"for their own reasons." If she were not dating, she would be missing the opposite sex and be lonely. Currently, she has two men whom she sees regularly. Mostly for dinner. Which means they take turns picking up the check. Sometimes she needs an escort for something or other because she does not like to go alone. She stated she was not interested in marriage, but "life is long, and I could change my mind." She grinned again.

Rose is at peace with herself. She has come to terms with who she is at this stage of her life and is living happily. Her mortality is on the horizon. She is neither anxious nor fearful of it.

— Patricia - 78 —

You met Patricia in the chapter "Busy, Busy, Busy." Remember, she's the one who "dumped" her husband when she was seventy-two, and is loving her single life. She thinks of herself as not over the hill, but as a foxy lady who is out there in the dating world giving and having a good time. Her attitude to her own mortality, her attitude to the aging process, her attitude toward life, and her spiritual makeup all have something to do with her "joie de vivre" at seventy-eight years old.

Patricia truly believes that she is going to live well into her nineties, even over 100. Why? Her mother died at ninety-eight. Her grandmother died at 100. Her aunt died at 102. (She discounts the fact that her dad died at seventy-six.) Her attitude as she expressed it with a crinkly smile, "I'm stuck on this planet for another thirty years or so. I might just as well enjoy it."

Patricia used the word "foxy" to describe her total persona. "Foxy" was not a word she created, but a word a "much" younger man said to her face when he and she met at a bar.

Patricia looks well *for her age*. (I hate that expression; that's why I italicized it.) She's had work done. She had a few facelifts. The last one was after she was got divorced—at seventy-three. She called it a "touch-up." She's had several dermatological treatments over the years, including liposuction to bring back some of her curvier lines. "I do what I feel I need to do, and what I can afford to make me look alive and well." Her hair is dyed a soft brown with blonde highlights. Her natural hair color is pepper and salt—75 percent gray and percent brown. "Not becoming ... it was too old-looking," she said.

Note, please, dear reader, she did not use the word "pretty," or even "attractive." When I brought that point up, she "corrected" me to say, "*Attractive* and *pretty* are in the eyes of the beholder, at any age. When I make changes to my appearance it makes me happier. I am sure my *happiness* with myself is reflected with my becoming more attractive or prettier in the eyes of the beholder. Everyone is attracted to a person who exudes happiness."

Patricia has a flexible attitude toward life. She has even a more flexible attitude toward her "age group." She believes in God. She believes that her life has been fated, and is fated until the day she dies. She goes to church fairly often. Since she cannot really change her fate, her attitude is why worry about it. This, she feels, gives her a flexibility to enjoy people no matter their age, their physical attributes, their personalities. She admitted there have been exceptions to this, of course.

— Virginia —

Everything in life is a trade-off. I am eighty-four years old. And yes, I feel it. Every bone in my body hurts from time to time. It's the weather. It's something I ate. I've given up trying to figure out what's going on in my body.

That's the downside of my growing old.

But the upside is that I feel better in some very important ways. I am freer today than I ever was in my whole life. I am financially freer. I am socially freer. I am sexually freer.

I don't have to answer to anybody. And I mean anybody! I do want what I want when I want it. And I go for it. I even approach men. I never did that when I was younger!

Since this is a book about sex (isn't that what you mean when you use the word "secrets" in your title?), you should write that I am sexually freer.

I cannot do the same gymnastics in bed that I could have done when I was younger. But I've made up for it by my enjoyment of it. I appreciate it when I get it...in whatever form it comes. I love to please a man. When was the last time you enjoyed pleasing someone else? It's a great feeling. It's actually a feeling of empowerment. I feel stronger, when I see I am making a man happy. No one in my family really needs me anymore. There is nothing I can do to make my kids, or my grandkids happy...except maybe give them money. They really don't need or want me on a one-to-one basis. That could be why I am such a "swinger." (Ginny smiled really broadly when she said "swinger.") I am involved now, with a guy my own age. If I outlive him, I will find myself another one. You can be sure of that. P.S. My kids and grandkids love to hear about my social life. They always kind of bring it up. That's the only thing they like to hear about me, I'm afraid. You can be sure they will buy your book.

To conclude, I want to return to the article I introduced at the beginning of this chapter:

"Is There a Limit To the Human Lifespan?"

Below the introduction to the question, the lead-in provided some background. It stated longevity seems to have topped out at about 120 years. The all-time verified age record was set by Jeanne Calment of France, who died in 1997 at age 122. However, the ranks of people older than 110 continue to grow. Below this lead-in were two articles written in response to the question.

The first response was by Brandon Milholland, co-author of several papers on aging and longevity and a research associate at a pharmaceutical consulting firm. He wrote "Yes - The Upper Limit Seems to be 125." "Yes, average life expectancy has increased, thanks to things like clean water, improved living conditions and modern medicine. But these improvements can only do so much, and eventually the body wears out."

The second response was written by Joon Yun, President of Palo Alto Investors and the $2 million founding donor of the National Academy of Medicine's Grand Challenge for Healthy Longevity. He wrote "No—The Key is Bioresilience"—meaning there was the possibility of biological inventions to increase maximum lifespan. New and emerging medical technologies might be able to slow aging to such an extent that not only will we live much longer, but we'll stay biologically "younger" well into what used to be our "old age."

So two experts disagree, and the debate continues. While the search for answers continues, and while the search continues, none of us should expect to live to 125. But we can and should pay attention to the flood of information provided to us to increase our lifespans.

Today, more than yesterday, more than last month, more than last year, we are offered ways to manage our longevity. We read, we hear, we are told, we can improve our old age, not only by extending it chronologically, but also improve our quality of life as we age. We read, we hear, we are told, we can maintain sexual function and needs to our very end.

Our ability to affect our lifespan is comforting and discomforting at the same time. We have choices to make. We have paths to try. We have expectations to fulfill.

As I sit here, writing this, I received a robo-call: "If you are a senior citizen, listen carefully to this message. Sign up for a medical alert system, because you are prone to need emergency lifesaving procedures."

I am looking forward to receiving a robo-call saying, "If you are a senior citizen, listen carefully to this message. Sign up for a medical alert system, because you are prone to need emergency lifesaving procedures. Also, sign up for our older folks cruise to Tahiti. We will cater to your individual medical, nutritional, and social needs, offer slow dancing, water aerobics, and lots of wonderful 'couch potato' entertainment. You will meet lots of like-minded folk and have the time of your life."

***

CHAPTER SIX
MONEY, MONEY, MONEY!

YOU MET LARRY IN AN EARLIER CHAPTER, "BUSY, BUSY, Busy," where you read how he met new women on the Internet. You read how much research and effort Larry was putting into meeting new women. I was visiting him for the first time since Peter died. It was the first time I visited him in Arizona. This is the rest of his story. And, sadly, it's not a pretty one.

Larry had lived pretty high on the hog...not rich, but on over $250,000 a year, when a restaurant meal in the higher-end restaurants in Manhattan cost no more than $30.00 a head.

But now, Larry is pretty much penniless. Between spending it on his lifestyle, his kids, and his divorces, he has little more than his Social Security to live on. That was the major reason he pulled up stakes in Manhattan and resettled in Scottsdale.

To continue his story. I asked him, "So, Larry, are you having fun?"

"No," said Larry. "When I meet someone and like her, the conversation almost immediately goes to how much money I have coming in every week. These women do not mince words. I am honest and tell them I have no money. They say sorry, but they are not interested in going further and getting involved with me."

Then, sighing, Larry goes on to say women he met have absolutely no interest in a man who has no money. They are asking nothing from the man in the future and even in the present. They are willing and able to support themselves and share in the expenses. But they have no interest in a guy...no matter how attractive, how intelligent, how loving the guy may be, unless he can keep up with their quality of life.

In short, at this older age, "What does love have to do with it?"

ALL ABOUT MONEY?

What does money have to do with moving a dating situation into the development of a relationship? Unfortunately, in our age group—everything. Everything may be an exaggeration, but the truth is that money plays a more important role in after sixty-five-year-old relationships than in relationships when we were young.

Underlying our choice to go beyond a first date and to move to the bonding in a relationship is our private answer to the question, HOW MUCH MONEY ARE YOU BRINGING TO THE TABLE?

Both men and women answer this question to themselves, just at different times, as that first date evolves or doesn't evolve into a mating relationship. That's the point of the illustration at the head of this chapter.

As the woman, you are sitting across the table from your first date with this rather nice fellow, you are sizing up the size of his wallet rather than (not to be crude about it) the size of his penis.

For the guy, the money issue comes later. When he sits across the table, he is deciding whether he finds the woman attractive. He is deciding "how she looks in bed." That's a direct quote from more than a few of my male interviewees.

This thought process was echoed always in my conversations with so many folks over sixty-five. They all have a keen interest in the other's money. It's simply a matter of timing.

WHAT'S LOVE GOT TO DO WITH IT?

Folks in their sixties, seventies, and eighties who tell me they are in a bonded relationship also tell me they are refusing to "tie the knot" and combine households. "Why?" I asked over and over again.

When we were younger, we and our dates were starting out and building careers. Basically, we both had nothing. Money was something we would or could work for together, as a team, as we built our life together. Even if we were stay-at-home mothers, we just knew that we were a team that were building our financial future together as we were building our family together.

But the younger generation is now marrying later. According to a U.S. census report, in the 1970s, about eight in ten married by the age of thirty. In 2016, that same percentage wasn't reached until age forty-five.

Marrying later means in all likelihood, each party has accumulated assets and/or started a business.

Today, we sign legal agreements that detail our financial arrangements. These documents do not signal an unromantic lack of trust, or suggest that one person is foreseeing an end to the union. These agreements are signed to protect the individual assets accumulated for the benefit of next of kin or others. They are called pre-nuptial or post-nuptial agreements if a legal marriage is involved. Today, they can simply be called a "Living Together Agreement."

For older folks, past sixty, we are looking toward preserving our quality of life, passing on some of our wealth to our family, and not having to worry about another person whom we have encountered later in our life. Agreements vary as to their specificity. Most speak to our assets, such as a business or real estate we own. Many include living-together financial contributions, like who pays for the food, or for travel, or for heat for the house. Or how the telephone bill should be divided.

Every married couple I interviewed had signed a pre-nuptial agreement. Except for one, come to think of it.

— Ronald And Melissa – Octogenarians —

Ronald and Melissa had been living together for about ten years. He had moved into her apartment, both believing two can live more cheaply than one. Ronald and Melissa took a trip to Las Vegas together, and at the ripe age of eighty-nine and eighty-three decided, on the spur of the moment, to "tie the knot." As Ronald said to me with a twinkle in his eye, "I decided to make an honest woman out of Melissa." Melissa then piped up, "That's because I kept crying over the years, when are you going to make an honest woman out of me? It took a trip to Las Vegas, and a good deal of liquor to pull it off." I loved the playful way they responded to my questioning. Recently, they told me they succumbed to pressure from their children and wrote up a post-nuptial agreement, primarily, as they both chimed in, to protect their children's inheritances.

— Bob – 76 —

Bob is sitting on his veranda overlooking his formal garden on a beautiful summer day. He just announced he put his house on the market for $20,000,000.00. While he doesn't go into details, he makes it quite clear he is successful in his business. He responds to my questions on money with, "I expect a woman to pay her own way when we travel together." When I ask him if he thought that were fair—after all, the chances are he is going to have much more money than most of his dates—he responds with a shrug: "Not 50-50, perhaps—*well*, I might pay for all the food."

He goes on, "I worked hard all my life, supported my wife, raised two kids, paid for their schooling. Now, I am no longer interested in taking financial care of a woman. She needs to participate fully in the relationship."

Then, in a rather telling way, he adds, "If I were willing to support a woman, I would have joined a dating website for younger folks and gotten myself a younger woman. But younger women would be a financial pain in the ass and I am through with that headache. Marrying a younger woman makes me feel as if I am willing to pay for services. For what other reason would she want an older guy?"

To soften his statement, he says, "It's not only money that keeps me from younger women. It's also that I want a companion, someone I can talk to, and I don't want to father any more children. I've been there, done that."

For Bob, I could tell money is a dealbreaker.

— **Paul – 75** —

I am standing around the hors d'oeuvre table at the Yale Club, munching on the sushi the club offers its members. Paul smiles at me and comes over. He leans a bit and says, "I am so sorry to hear of Peter. He was such a nice fellow. I remember playing tennis with him...he was such a gentleman." Then he looks at me directly and says, "Eleanor, you are still a beautiful woman, how are you doing?"

I say pretty well. Am dating again. In fact, Paul, I am engaged to be married. I show Paul my engagement ring and tell him, Edward (whom he knew from the club) and I are planning our wedding.

Paul, looking a bit startled, says, "I have been divorced for twenty-five years and I have had a girlfriend for fifteen years since then." It was my turn to look startled. "Fifteen years, a girlfriend? Not marriage? Why didn't you guys get married?" Paul answers, "Money issues are too confusing. I don't need the pressure, and neither does she."

"I can't afford her. She can't afford me. She gets a pension to live on. I scrape by on my earnings. Our Social Security checks would go down if we got married."

I asked, "Do you ever bring her to the club?"

"Sometimes," he answered. "But not that often."

— Susan and Anthony - 71 & 68 —

"I am not a rich woman," says Sue. Sue is living on a pension she received from the city, as a city employee of over twenty years. She lives in a rent-stabilized one-bedroom apartment in the 30s in New York City. Sue is very middle-class, financially.

Sue is seventy-one. She never married. But she claims to have had several long-term relationships. Anthony, sixty-eight years old, moved into her apartment three years ago. Anthony has less money coming in than Sue. But like Sue, he gets guaranteed income—from his trucking company.

We have an understanding. Anthony pays his way. He shares in everything, even down to the phone bill. He brings in less a month than I do. But I don't care. He has to carry his weight, right down the middle.

I have no intention of supporting a man. Period. I've worked too hard. Yes, I walked away from a few relationships when I saw that the guy could be a drag. Bob's income is guaranteed. So, I don't have to worry.

I agree with your line of questioning. At our age of Dating and Mating, "What does love have to do with it?"

— David – 72 —

I was introduced to David through his son, Ken. Ken is one of my financial advisers. I told Ken I was writing a book on Dating and Mating of folks after sixty-five. He said I had to talk to his dad. His dad, David, was divorced from Ken's mom when David was fifty. So technically, he should not be in this book. But Ken insisted, saying that his dad went through the money thing big-time and could be used as an example. So I called David, now seventy-two, who is living with his second life (and by the way, Ken's stepmother) somewhere in a retirement community in Florida. He was happy to come to the phone. He was happy to share his story. He said he was "stupid" not to have signed a pre-nuptial agreement. But at that time, it wasn't as popular as it is now. He and his current wife ended up in couples' therapy because of money problems. After eight months of couples' therapy, they decided to sign a post-nuptial agreement. According to David, it was either a post-nuptial or another divorce. They agreed that another divorce would have been worse. The money issues were not about the "big" things like separate assets or bank accounts, but contributions to the household. In other words, who pays for living costs, and how much.

They now have separate phone landlines, with different phone numbers, because she made so many more phone calls than he.

She shops for her own groceries. He shops for his own groceries. He cooks and eats most of his own meals. Same for her. His wife wanted this arrangement because she always wanted to go out for dinner. She resented cooking at home. This way, she was forcing him to determinate the cost-benefit of their going out for dinner, versus buying the food, cooking it, and eating separately at home.

When they go out to a restaurant, if he picks the restaurant, or if they agree on the restaurant, he will pick up the check, always. "I am still an old-fashioned boy at heart," he said. "**But,**" he said, emphasizing the "but" by raising his voice, "if she picks out the restaurant and it's her usual very expensive choice, then she has to pay me back her half of the meal, including tip."

We each have our own car. So, maintenance is not an issue. But when we shared a car, it was hell on earth. You know, figuring out how much gas she used. How much I used, and so on. It just got out of hand.

So, we wrote up a post-nuptial agreement. We had the advantage of living together for about two years, so we knew what the trigger issues were. We paid two separate attorneys anyway. We both knew this had to be a legal document to make it work.

Now our marriage is on track. We settle up every month. She keeps the "books." But we pretty much know what's going on. It's just been codified.

How do I justify this, you ask? Look, this is my second marriage. I am retired. I did not want any headaches the second time around. My second wife is, or would like to be, high-maintenance. Well, sorry, that's not what I had in mind when I married her.

I did not ask to speak to his wife. But I think that if I did, she would have complained that she didn't realize she'd married such a cheapskate.

But I left it at that. I am not in the business of getting into the middle of what works for senior folks who have married later in their lives. I am simply describing the landscape of mating as seniors as it is presented to me.

— Michelle - 75 —

Michelle comes from a moneyed family. Although her last name is innocuous, when you hear her maiden name, you say to yourself, "Oh, yes!"

At seventy-five years old, Michelle claims not to be dating anymore. She simply hangs around with a few older guys...guys whom she has known for years, whom she says she "can trust."

Money has been an issue for me, it seems, my entire life. The minute men would hear my name, I just knew they put me in a different category. But it got worse as I got older. Really. Once my dates were over sixty-five. I found myself dating retirees. These retirees seem to be much more concerned with money. Not only with their financial condition. They are much more curious about my financial condition. Maybe it's all those ads you see on TV that have made them nervous. You know, the ones that are asking a person if he or she has enough for retirement? It's disgusting, in my opinion, how these "financial advisors," or whatever they call themselves, try to scare folks into giving them their hard-earned money.

Anyway, back to my point. It was so bad that my stock answer was that I received only a small amount of money to live on from a trust. And that I had no, absolutely no, control over the money I received. The fact that I lived on 5th Avenue in New York City didn't help very much, but at least I did limit the damage, somewhat.

I don't know if this really fits into your book, or not. But I can repeat, "the moment I started dated retired men, the worse it got."

MONEY ISSUES CAN BE DEALBREAKERS

"Too confusing" is a rather apt expression for how our accumulation of assets (a really good thing) has become something of an albatross when we are talking about marrying the person with whom we have bonded.

Enter "pre-nuptial" agreements; enter "post-nuptial" agreements; enter "living together" agreements. Enter lawyers. Enter the cost of lawyers. Enter the thought that money is the single most divisive factor against the formation of a bonded relationship.

There was a time, many moons ago, when pre-nuptial agreements were between monarchs and royalty who married. It was a clarification and a recognition of family property assets. If, for example, you were Eleanor of Aquitaine, as Queen of Aquitaine, you personally owned a major chunk of today's France. You married the King of France, you would have (as she did) written an agreement to retain title to your land of Aquitaine. So even though Eleanor of Aquitaine became Queen of France and then later Queen of England (another story), behind it all, she still retained her own personal ownership of that original chunk of land called Aquitaine.

At that time, pre-nuptial agreements were written for purposes of heredity, which we call today "estate planning." Divorce was not an issue because in our more Catholic world of Christianity, there was no divorce, only an annulment from the Pope.

Slowly, starting with King Henry VIII, his break with the Pope, and the start of the Anglican Church, annulment was no longer necessary to get free of your spouse and to re-marry. You no longer needed the Pope's approval. You could be divorced by the government.

Slowly, but surely, divorce became more prevalent. As the government had given certain rights to the spouse, rich men needed to protect their assets.

It was considered unfair when a person who had accumulated all the wealth should be forced to give too much of it away just because of marriage. Then, it was pretty much of a one-way street, written by the man who had the wealth for the intended bride to sign if she wanted a ring on her finger.

Hence the word "pre-nuptial," meaning before the marriage.

In my childhood, I hardly heard of pre-nuptial agreements. When I did, it was because some very rich man was involved in divorce, and my parents read a snippet of it in the newspapers.

The pre-nuptial (pre-marriage) agreement was a legal document drawn up to withstand the scrutiny of the court. Although it need not be drawn up by a lawyer, it quickly became clear to everyone (especially the lawyers) that it took a legal mind to protect us from unclear interpretations of what we actually need.

MY STORY

In fact, the issue of money was probably the determinate factor why Edward and I failed to get married.

Shortly after my encounter with Paul at the Yale Club, Edward and I decided to write up a pre-nuptial agreement. Both of us had been married, he for fifty years, me for forty-four years, but neither of us had had any interest in forming any kind of formal financial living agreement with our spouses. In those days, we just argued it out. But we knew it was a common thing to do in today's world. He hired a lawyer. I hired a lawyer, even though I am a practicing attorney. We each paid for our own retainers.

We ended up with dueling drafts of agreements. Keeping our assets separate was easy. What did us in was the sharing of household and living expenses.

I wanted a joint bank account where we would each contribute a lump sum to cover all our living and social expenses for the month.

He wanted lots of living expenses spelled out in the agreement. For example, there was the issue of household cleaning and laundry help. I was paying for cleaning and laundry help twice a week, a holdover from my pre-widow days when I was running a home. He wanted written he would pay only up to one-half of household cleaning and laundry costs, and only for two times a month.

This bickering was not between Edward and me directly, but between our attorneys! On billable hours.

We both finally gave up trying to figure out how to apportion our finances as a married couple and agreed to live together without being married. Simply, duke it out as we did with our deceased spouses. So our wedding ceremony became a "commitment party."

That did not seem to help the matter any. Eventually, over a period of months, he simply said he wanted to maintain the relationship as it was. He would not give up his apartment. He declared his love for me, but stated he just was unable to give up his apartment and move in. We would continue to live separately but continue bonded.

I returned his ring but continued seeing him. I still cared deeply for him. He was still the same person.

But my bonded relationship with Edward simply died under its own weight.

I re-entered the world of dating and found someone new to whom I was attracted. I lost my attraction for Edward. My sex switch had turned off. He was upset. Our relationship morphed into "let's just be good friends," and he continued to call me every morning to say "hi." That was our relationship until the day he died, about four years later.

To this day I blame the lawyers, and the money issues the pre-nuptial agreement was trying to "resolve," that drove an irreparable wedge into our relationship.

— Arlene - 74 —

Arlene was left impoverished after her husband died. It's as simple as that. She was sixty-eight when her husband died. He was ten years older than she, and died at seventy-nine. They had a lovely house just outside of Los Angeles, in San Diego, California. Their only son was married, with kids of his own. She put their house on the market. It didn't sell. She lowered the price of her house. It didn't sell. The house had been paid off. She needed the cash desperately. It is now a few years later. Arlene was seventy-four when I interviewed her. She had gone through all the savings, which she stated was not very much, and spent all her husband's life insurance money. She was down to "the wire," as she put it.

I know what my problem is. I am used to a high lifestyle. My family lived comfortably. We traveled. We ate out rather often. I could maintain myself without watching every penny.

But now I am living a different life. The men I attract have as little as I do. They bring nothing to the table. If I get involved again, it's going to have to be a guy who has a few bucks in his pocket. That's why I am all alone now. I am lonely. Frankly, I feel sorry for myself. And at times, I get angry at my dead husband. I am unwilling to go to the "Y" to meet a man who is using the "Y." He can be nice-looking, be in good health, be charming, but if a man can't afford a private gym, or take me out to a decent restaurant, or dress well, there's no reason for me to let myself go to the next step. I will only be sorry in the long run that I hooked up with him in the first place.

So I read a lot. This interview is giving me some ideas about trying to develop myself. Maybe I can make some money, some good money at my age. I need to get off this treadmill. Maybe when I read your book, I will get energized to do something with the rest of my life.

— **Phyllis - 80** —

Phyllis simply stated she did not make a move without sizing up the guy's ability to pay. Including his ability to support her—should it come to that.

She had been sizing men up like that all her life, as a matter of fact. That's how she was brought up. Phyllis is eighty years old. She was married and widowed twice. She is in a long-term relationship now with a man slightly younger than she. She doubts that they will ever marry.

I am of the generation before the sexual or women's revolution, whatever you want to call it. Pre-Woodstock. I went to an elite all-girls college. One of the Seven Sisters, if you know what I am talking about. Not one of our graduating class went to graduate school. There was not a single pre-med student in my class. We are all concerned about our MRS. You know, getting engaged before we graduated. Graduate with a ring on our fingers. Our role was to be the strength of the family. Raise the kids while dad went to work to support us. We believed we had the most important role in family life. We were the disciplinarians from day to day. We imparted culture and cultural values to our children. We were the ones who taught them manners, about life, about everything. Dad was the gallant guy out there working his butt off to keep a roof over our heads.

And yes, we were supposed to be virgins.

This was all before the pill.

So it was really a shock for me when I re-entered the dating world at seventy-four years old. I heard that single women were paying for the man's dinner. I heard that they were splitting the check. I even saw them split the check. To me that was a horror!

I saw single women giving their calling cards to single men.

Well, Eleanor, I'm really not complaining. It has not prevented me from dating or mating as you are calling it.

I am actually having a wonderful widowhood. The men I meet and have met always pay for the dinner. We do not meet over a coffee. It's always a dinner. A nice romantic meal in a "white-tablecloth" restaurant. I expect my date, at any age, to act with civility and class. I have my standards.

And I am happy to say that all the men I have dated to date have behaved themselves properly.

I reciprocate, as a lady should. That means I invite them to dinner at my home, or to my club. I might buy tickets to take a man to theater with me.

Obviously, I am financially independent. I do not count a man's money. I count the way he handles his money. I expect him to follow the rules. The rules of dating and mating.

As I fully expect to die single, I do not even give a thought to a financial arrangement between my significant other and me. No pre-nuptials. No contracts. I feel sorry for the younger folk today. They have made life so very complicated for themselves, and now have to live with it.

— **Yvette and Charles – Septuagenarians** —

Yvette and Charles met on a senior singles website. I spoke to them both together in Yvette's living room. Yvette was known as a cabaret singer. She, at seventy-six, is a large woman. Not fat, but large. She was tall and probably a size sixteen. Charles is quite a big guy *for his age*. He looks as if he is at least 6'2". He demurred, saying that he used to be a "good" 6'2" but lost a bit of ground. They both agreed that a major reason they are now a couple is that "he was big enough for me," said Yvette. And Charles chimed in, "Yvette is a woman whom I can find easily. She is a voluptuous woman."

Both are religious, in the sense they go to church together every Sunday. Both said they would have preferred marriage, but their financial issues made matters too expensive.

There was the fact that they would have to give up their separate Social Security checks if they were legally married. There were different kinds of marital deductions depending upon whether you were single or married. Yvette belonged to a country club. When her husband died, she was awarded "Widow's Status." That meant she had to pay only ½ the dues required of her when she was a family member—when her husband was alive. That, in her mind and in reality, was a substantial savings.

Both claimed that they decided practicality was more important than their wish to be legally bonded.

Yvette said, "When we were young, we needed to be married, because our newborn children needed the stability of parents and a legitimate last name. We don't have that issue now. We can do the practical thing... the thing that works for us in our relationship."

Charles chimed in, "Look at the young folks today. More and more of them are breeding together, having children together, and not getting married. Don't ask me why, but the institution of marriage seems to be fading—for the old and the young alike."

The long and the short of it, is the "MONEY MATTERS." As an older single citizen, however you end up dealing with it, you need to be alert to that elephant in the room—MONEY!

***

CHAPTER SEVEN

KIDS ARE THE NEW IN-LAWS

I F YOU THINK DATING AND MATING IN YOUR SIXTIES, seventies, eighties, and nineties is turning your life topsy-turvy, nothing will make that clearer than this chapter, "Kids are the New In-Laws."

This chapter is where we talk about our age, society's attitude towards our age, and the shift from parenting to our children's parenting of us. If I present the case properly, you should be able to understand where your children are coming from—what they are thinking about, worrying about you, their single parent—dating and mating in your sixties and later. For those of you who never had kids, please substitute other members of your family—like sisters, brothers, nieces, nephews, and so on.

It is said, "Understanding the problem is half the cure." If you understand your family's reluctance to embrace your dating and mating, you will be better prepared to handle the matter with strength and dignity. At least you will not be caught "flat-footed" as I was.

WHAT IS OUR TIME?

There comes a time in our lives when we are freer of our responsibilities to others, can spend more money on ourselves, and have more time to pursue our personal choices. We are financially freer, morally freer, and emotionally freer—to be who we want to be and do what we want to do. If we are married or partnered at this time, then this time belongs to the two of us. If we are single at this time, then this time should become the easiest time for us to date and mate.

Our time occurs when we are free of responsibilities to our children, our younger siblings, our parents, and when we are free from societal restrictions. This is our time of life where we should be able to live, love, and be selfishly true to ourselves. This should be "Our Time."

AT WHAT AGE DOES "OUR TIME" BEGIN?

Remember the expression, "Life Begins at Forty?"

That was true for our parents' generation. By forty, most of our parents lost their parents because life expectancy for males was in their sixties, and for females, in their seventies. Our parents married younger, had children earlier, and earned their freedom earlier to do what they could afford without the constraints of children.

Today, our children are leaving home later, getting married later, and having their children later. Birthing after fifty years old has been growing. According to *Parents' Magazine*, births by women who were pregnant between the ages of fifty and fifty-four increased by more than 165% from 2000 to 2013.

Nowadays, when we jokingly ask the question, "When does life begin?" The answer is more than likely to be based upon what is going on in our life now, than at any particular age.

SOCIETY'S INVOLVEMENT IN "OUR TIME"

Government regulations, as well as the absence of government regulations, reflect a society's attitude towards its people.

Here, in the United States, we have divided our people into legal categories based on our chronological age. We have the legal categories of "minor," "adult," and "senior citizen."

MINORS TO ADULTS

Our government begins to treat us as adults somewhere between the ages of sixteen and twenty-one. Until then we are legally considered "minors."

As a minor, we are legally prohibited from exercising our freedom to own certain things, or use things, or do certain activities.

As a minor, we are prohibited from obtaining a driver's license until sixteen. We cannot buy or be served liquor until eighteen to twenty-one. We are restricted from buying firearms until we are eighteen. We cannot open and maintain our own bank account until eighteen. We cannot vote until we are eighteen.

In many states, we cannot marry before the age of eighteen without the consent of parents. Nor can we have an abortion without the consent of a parent.

It is not until our twenties that society allows us to fully participate in adult society, without any limitations because of our chronological age. Once we are deemed adults, our adult status continues until we die.

ADULTS TO SENIORS

The concept of "senior citizen" is a relatively new one.

Starting with the New Deal of the 1930s, society tacked on an additional category to adulthood, now called "senior citizens." We do not lose any benefits of adulthood, but are provided additional benefits when we reach our sixties.

In the 1930s, our government's act of providing Social Security payments to citizens over sixty-five began the seismic change from older folks' dependency on our younger and stronger children to more personal independence.

Thanks to Lyndon Johnson's Great Society legislation in the 1960s, folks over sixty-five are guaranteed health care.

The U.S. Code of Federal Regulations of the '70s stated an employer could no longer force retirement or otherwise discriminate based on age against an individual because he or she is seventy years or older. Today, there is no limit to the age when we must stop working.

Alongside our improving status as senior citizens, private businesses have caught on that there is a special market for seniors. Businesses offer more perks to seniors than to any other category. Movie theatres offer senior entrance discounts. Travel organizations offer senior discounts. Your local supermarket may offer a senior citizen shopping discount day. And so on.

Even though we seniors have been gaining benefits, society has not put any limitations on us because of our age. For example, once we receive our driver's license, we never lose it because we are too old to drive. We are never forced to stop marrying because we are "too old."

Up to now, you have read that by our sixties, we are free from personal family obligations, giving us more freedom to be who we are and do what we want. You have read that our government is providing funds and legislation to help us be financially free. You have read how businesses, eager to tap our senior citizen class, offer us perks and discounts.

This period of our so-called new freedom, thanks to decreased obligations and increased benefits, has come to be called "Our Time."

So, read on, and find out why you need to see the problem we have when we are dating and mating in our sixties and beyond.

OUR TIME

When I asked widowed and divorced seniors how they felt about being single, they answered, to a person, "Pretty damn good," or "A hell of a lot better than I thought." "Why?" I asked. The answer was, "Because I have my independence and my privacy."

Later in life divorces, dubbed "silver" or "gray" divorces, have more than doubled since 1990 among couples who are sixty-five and older, making up 25% of all Americans who divorce after the age of fifty. I interviewed several folks who divorced after more than forty years of marriage. The reason they gave was that they each believed they had enough time ahead of them to reset their clocks, and to enjoy life. They were willing to put up with the extreme difficulties of obtaining a divorce in the expectation they had future years ahead of them where they could see themselves happier.

Suffice it to say that none of my interviewees ever mentioned their desire to live with their children, now or in the future. In fact, they expressed horror at the thought. They all expressed a preference for some sort of senior living, independent of their family. If not alone, completely independent, then in some sort of community environment. But never with the kids.

It's quite amazing to realize that in most of the world today, parents and adult children and their children's family continue to live under one roof.

I interviewed no single senior who lived under the same roof as his or her children. The closest I came to it was where the single, divorced dad in his seventies elected to live in an in-law apartment attached to his son's family home in Seattle, Washington. But he still maintained himself very independently, coming and going as he pleased. He was dating and maintaining his privacy about it.

Folks over sixty believe they have the best of all possible worlds because they have time, assets, and most importantly, their independence and privacy.

However, they are forgetting the inevitable fact that there is a shifting of balance of power between them and their children.

CHILDREN TAKE CONTROL

There has always been the question, "When do the kids start making decisions for their mom or dad?"

I hesitate to use the expression, "Balance of Power," but I believe it is the most apt expression I can think of to illustrate the underlying point of this chapter and how it affects our dating and mating.

There is a shift in the balance of power within family relationships—when the child becomes the parent and the parent becomes the child. It's just a question of time, at what age, and in what manner we begin to see that shift.

Before the 1930s, it was commonly accepted that the family took care of their aging parents. Folks had large families. Unless extremely wealthy, parents often moved in with a child or children. Our aging was a slow and hidden process, going on within each family, behind closed doors.

It is no longer a natural slow process that occurs because you are living under one roof— one that involves familial, internal adjustments. Now it can involve rather cantankerous arguments involving not only family, but friends of the family, going more and more public into lawyers, guardianships, and legal decisions by courts...of what should be strictly family affairs.

When we begin dating, it becomes quite clear there is a tug of war between parent and child.

KIDS ARE THE NEW IN-LAWS

Be prepared. "Our Time" does not mean we are free to do whatever we want. If we are single in our sixties, our time for dating and mating is now. You may be living alone. Maybe in a senior community. Maybe in an assisted living facility. But your children, out there on their own, will be watching you—even from afar.

Their "antenna" suddenly goes up when they hear their single senior parent is dating. It can happen at any time, anywhere—even over the phone, even though the kids and parent live far from each other.

By and large, they initially mouth words expressing happiness that you are Out There. They want you to enjoy your life. They want you to have good times. They want you to have your own company for the movies, restaurants. They want you to have someone to travel with. They are quietly delighted that they don't have to drag you along on their activities.

You would think they would be happy that you met someone who you want to live with, perhaps marry, and who wants to live with you, and perhaps marry. It would make sense that as you age, you would not be entirely alone. There would be someone else in your life, who would be a companion to you.

Likewise, we may think we have a better relationship with our children because we have found a companion. We are emotionally less dependent on them. We are less sensitive to whether they call or do not call; whether they remember our birthday; and so on.

Our children's concern becomes obvious at our mating state...when you've been seeing someone for a while. The children, or family as the case may be, know they cannot stop their parent from dating. At least, no one of my interviewees admitted they were actually stopped by their kid from dating. The trouble begins when we are at the mating stage.

They feel obliged to look after you—to protect you and your interests. Which, of course, are their interests.

Every child of a single parent with whom I talked (which were not that many of course...because I was talking to their parents) expressed happiness that they saw their parent dating. But, *well,* when it came to mating—that was another story.

This shift has played itself out in court. There has been a rise in court requests for guardianship power by children over parents. Guardianship is a legal term designating a person who is "lawfully invested with the power and charged with the obligation of taking care of and managing the property and rights of a person who because of age, understanding or self-control, is considered incapable of administering his or her own affairs."

The child seeking guardianship over a parent goes to court to apply for guardianship. The court has and uses its authority to appoint a court lawyer to represent the parent. In the last ten years, there has been a commensurate rise in a parent retaining his own private attorney and appearing in court to oppose the guardianship. Matters between parent and child can and often do get ugly. Nobody in his seventies, eighties, or nineties really likes to hear he is incompetent and lacks the capacity to make his own decisions. Especially when he is single and dating!

Even though there is a ton of money—enough to go around—families have still gone after the surviving partner to prevent the partner from inheriting their father's estate. A notorious and sad case is the story of Anna Nicole Smith and her battle to share in the billion-dollar estate of her husband, who died in 2005 at ninety years old. His children sued to deny her any inheritance. You may recall that the case went up to the Supreme Court of the United States because of the convoluted jurisdictional issues of the argument. As of 2017, the case has not been resolved, even though Anna Nicole Smith passed away in 2007.

This stuff can get very nasty. Make no doubt about it.

MY STORY

I met Edward through friends who knew us both from the Yale Club. It soon got around the club that Edward and I were a couple. Edward was eighty years old at the time. I was seventy-four. We both were widowed.

Edward has four children, ranging from their forties to their early fifties. Three girls and one boy. When Edward and I started dating, I was introduced to them all. Edward was sure to include me in their lives, in his life with them. According to Edward, they liked me very much—I reminded them of their late mom. I felt very comfortable with them. I felt very simpatico. I loved being incorporated into their lives. I am an only child. I have no siblings, no brothers or sisters to involve me in their lives. I have no nieces or nephews. The fact that Edward had all this family stuff going on around him was an enrichment to me. I attended birthday parties for his grandchildren. I even met his mother.

I knew he wanted them to like me. I could feel he was hoping for their approval. But that didn't bother me. In fact, I welcomed it. Since I just felt that they genuinely liked me, and approved of me, I felt as if my life was enriched.

About nine months after we met, Edward and I agreed to get married. We got engaged— ring and all. Suddenly, immediately, his children expressed their disapproval of our relationship going any further. According to Edward, it was the three girls who did not want a change in our relationship—meaning, "Dad, continue dating her, but no more co-mingling than that." His son's reaction was different. It was much more of a hands-off attitude, like, "Dad, do what you want."

The girls won. Edward succumbed to their wishes or fears, or whatever you want to call it. Two weeks before our marriage (which had morphed into a commitment ceremony), he sat me down, and said he couldn't go through with any ceremony. He said he could not live together with me and wanted to continue our relationship as it was. He insisted he was bonded to me. He just couldn't go any farther. He wanted to continue living apart. As I stated in "Money, Money, Money," he broke off our marriage plans, begging me to keep our relationship the way it was. I was devastated. It was the most demeaning experience I had in my seventy years of life.

Our relationship went from love to friendship. Three years later, we were still close enough that I was involved in his passing away, visiting him in the hospital as he lay dying.

At one point, since his death, one of his daughters kind of apologized to me by saying, "Eleanor, it was not you. It was never you. We always loved you. We just didn't want dad to get married."

I wonder how they will feel when their kids say the same thing to them when they are seniors looking for love and companionship.

What came out of their rejection of me is this book. I realized that a woman, even as late as in her seventies, back in the dating and mating world, was on a journey she could not have envisioned. It is a story worth sharing as a guide to everyone who has entered this world or is considering entering this world. I saw I needed to write this book, to take you on my journey with me.

TOM'S COMMENTS

I am told by a married friend that my experience with Edward and his family is typical of his friends.

Tom is a retired dentist, living with his wife in Florida in a gated community—not a retirement community, but with a large group of retired folks. They have a communal dining room where he hears all sorts of dating and mating stories over dinner. When he heard my story, and that I was writing this book, he simply shook his head and said, "That's daughters for you." Tom explained that dinner conversation often included senior male retirees who had live-in partners. The men complained their daughters were constantly calling them, criticizing the relationship, trying to break it up. His female partner would either just keep nodding her head, or sometimes chime in to say that the relationship between the parents and children was like a war zone—sometimes quiet, but very tense, nonetheless.

Tom continued to say that it was the girls who put the kibosh on the mating, not the boys—exactly my story.

So I asked, what is the underlying motivation? Is it about inheritance? Are girls more afraid their new mother-in-law would spend it all, or steal it somehow, and they would be left in the cold?

Tom said that if this were the underlying motivation, wouldn't sons also have the same worries? They would also feel entitled to their dad's inheritance. If it were only about money, then dad's "new" relationship with another woman was an interference with their expected legacy, whether son or daughter.

Tom said for girls it was not just about, or only about, money. Daughters simply think that their fathers are naïve, innocent of a woman's need to be boss. Men are easy to control. They just want sex. They remember their mom was the boss of the family. Daughters want to be in charge, to take care of their dads in the same way that their mom did. Now they are. They don't want to see a stranger coming in at the 11th hour and controlling their lovely old dad. The daughters know best.

I agree with Tom's assessment. This is not a scientific discovery but provides perhaps a window into the structure of the American family. We have become a matriarchal society. The woman, the mother, is the central figure in the house. She is the boss of the family. Daughters understand that.

They saw it in their parents' relationship. They see it in their own married relationship. They don't want to see it in their dad's new relationship.

— Mark —

I am sitting with Mark in his moderately-furnished living room. He is short and portly. Not much to look at. He has neuropathy of his left foot. He is a recent widower and is dating "like crazy." Every morning, he has his secretary check two dating websites. She brings to his attention women whom she thinks he should check out. Sort of a morning briefing.

The phone rings. He takes the call. It's from his forty-something-year-old son. I hear Mark say to his son that he met another woman whom is he taking to the theater that coming Saturday.

After the call, I ask Mark how often he communicates with his son about his dating. Mark, looking surprised, says "as often as something happens." Then he goes on with a smile, "My son is living vicariously through me. He really wants to know if I am getting laid." I followed up with asking whether he cared what his son thought about his possibility of living with another woman or getting married. He responded that he had already checked it out with his son, and he has already placed some of his liquid assets into an irrevocable trust. "How about your apartment?" I asked. "You own your apartment, don't you?"

He said, yes, and that is his problem. He is not willing to put his apartment in a trust with his son as trustee. "Why?" I asked. He looked a little sheepish, and said, "I don't trust my son completely. He could very well take charge, put me away somewhere, and move in here with his family." I said, "But, that's not likely, is it?" "No," he responded, but "I heard stories from friends that when the kids start getting control of finances, at some point they feel justified in simply taking everything. I have friends in their eighties who are now in court over this very thing. Their kids—usually just one of them—gets greedy, finds some bastard of a lawyer who tries to get the kid guardianship over his mom or dad. I am not going to allow even a smidgen of that thought to enter my kid's head. So I am not putting anything else into a trust—especially my apartment."

ASSISTED LIVING STORY

I am sitting in front of the Director of an Assisted Living Center in the Bronx. The Center consists of a complex of four buildings containing assisted living facilities, as well as over two hundred independent housing units with support service. The age range is from the early sixties to their oldest resident, who was turning 105 at the time. Women outnumber men three to one. The Director stated that that number is moving more to two to one, as recent tours of prospective residents indicate.

I introduce myself as a researcher on dating and mating after Medicare. The Director smiles at me, and says, "You've come to the right place. This is Grossinger's in the Bronx." Grossinger's was a famous hotel in the Catskill mountains of New York State, until its closure in 1986.

The Director told me that while married couples come to the facility together, about 95% of their residents are single by the time they arrive. The great majority of the new residents are brought by a child or other family member.

Asked if the new residents entered the facility willingly, without pressure, the Director responded that the facility can accept only folks who are cognizant of their environment, their surroundings, and have their faculties about them. This is not a nursing home. The seniors may have trouble caring for themselves physically, but in all other ways are aware and informed. The answer then is, "Yes." The selection of the facility was a family decision with the prospective resident in complete agreement.

We turn to the Director's comment on Grossinger's, and I ask the question, bluntly, "What goes on sexually at the Center?"

The Director says there are plenty of sexual goings-on. She tells me about the couple that fell in love at the Center, both in their seventies. They were married here, and now live together in one apartment. When I asked who came to the wedding, the director said that there were no children on either side. A younger sister and a younger brother showed up.

She goes on to say that the staff monitors developing relationships very closely. She says, also, she informs the family about it. "Why?" I ask. "Is it a matter of health?" "No," she laughed, "it is probably a healthy thing to do." She said the families do not want any real entangling alliances. It could lead to marriage. It could lead to loss of control. They want their parent safe. Other than providing basic comforts, their parent's social life is not really a concern for them. It's only about safety.

I pushed somewhat further by asking, what control do the children have over their parent at this point? Not much, was the Director's answer. They do not have guardianship, if that's what you mean. The parent does not need a guardian. S(he) is fully capable of making appropriate choices. It's simply a matter of "pressure." If you want to be nice about it, call it "loving pressure." They couch their disapproval of the parent's socializing in a variety of ways, anywhere from putting the other person down to downright threats of removal from the facility.

— Rose and Her Sisters —

I am talking to Rose, a friend who lives in Southern California. She has two sisters and one brother. Rose is in her seventies, re-married for the past fifteen years. Dad, in his nineties, just got re-married. And there was "nothing" they could do about it.

How did that happen? He married his assisted living woman of thirteen years. She started out as paid assistant living help, by the day, when her dad was in his seventies. She was around thirty years younger than he. Over the years the relationship morphed into day and night. Obviously no longer in her dad's employ, the assistant was living with, and being supported by, her dad. The girls accepted it, of course, because it saved their dad money. He could continue living in his home without being a burden on them.

Surprise. One day, their dad called to say they got married. Rose sort of shrugged her shoulders and stated, "What could we do about it? It was a fait accompli." Unsaid in that conversation was a fact of which I was quite aware. He had savings in the six figures. She had nothing.

"Did they write a post-nuptial?" I asked Rose. She said that she didn't know, but none of them asked their dad. Besides, California is a community property state. Everything is 50-50, almost no matter what. There would be no purpose in signing anything, especially after the fact.

So, beware, as your dating turns into mating, you are going to hit unexpected pitfalls—namely, your family and your prospective mate's family are involved in your journey, one way or another. Your understanding that kids may step in and apply brakes to your relationship moving forward is half the battle to a successful move from dating to mating.

***

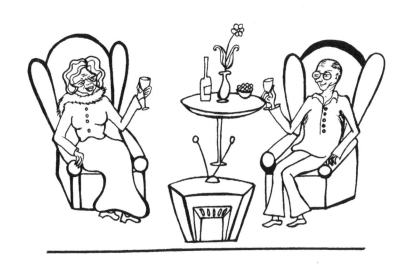

CHAPTER EIGHT
FIFTY SHADES
OF RELATIONSHIPS

Y OU HAVE BEEN ON A JOURNEY WITH ME. IN THE
dating section you read what other seniors are experiencing
in their sixties, seventies, eighties, and nineties. In the mating section
you read what issues seniors have encountered when they try to form
a relationship.

Finally, here, we are going to see what a relationship looks
like among older couples. The title of this chapter, "Fifty Shades Of
Relationships," is not meant to be a joke. We are going to see in our
later years that our sexual chemistry with another person takes many
forms of bonding, more innovative than the bonding of our younger
counterparts.

OUR MATING DIFFERS FROM OUR PARENTS

In previous chapters, you read about the differences between our parents and us in our attitudes to our sexuality and to our mortality. Now, we need to clarify the difference between our parents and us toward mating, forming a relationship, establishing a sexual bond with another person.

Prior to the 1960s, society saw the world of relationships as divided into two parts: Those who were married, and those who were not. Those who were married were in a relationship. Those who were not married, but were a couple for one reason or another, were not socially acceptable. If society acknowledged that these non-married people were in a relationship—that is, two people living together, or admitting to being a couple with a child in common but living apart—it was either sinful (if you were religious), or a pitiful state of affairs. The arrangement put the woman in a pathetic and weak position, undeserving of respect. It was unfair to the child. The child was deemed "illegitimate" at best, and a "bastard" at worst. For our parents' generation, and into the 1960s, an unmarried relationship was a sorry state of affairs.

Then, defining a relationship between two people was easy. If you were married, you were in a relationship. If you were not married, you were not. You were in something else. Marriage was proof.

The legal state of marriage as proof of a relationship began to break down in the 1960s. Slowly, but surely, people began to bond together and live together unmarried, with respect from society. These were folks who continued to work, and hold jobs. The stigma of not being married began to fade away as more and more women entered the workplace, and became better able to support themselves. A perfect sign of this was the phenomenon of women who did not change their last names to adopt the name of the father of their children, even if legally married. So, society began to accept that, say, Mary Smith, who might be married or not married to John Brown, had children who were named with Brown as their surname. It has not yet taken hold in the United States for parents to include the mother's surname with the dad's surname, hyphenated or not, as it has in some European countries. The point is, however, that women were making their own choice whether or not to allow society to see them as married or unmarried. Until then, marriage included a public statement of a name change for the woman. Today, the neutral abbreviation of "Ms." is often used instead of "Mrs." by married women who want to keep their legal status private.

In the 1950s and 1960s, it was the need to have sex, to procreate, to start a family that triggered the relationship called marriage. Today, parenting alone has become more of the triggering factor to legalize the relationship in the form of marriage. Our younger folk, who are in the childbearing age, as a rule, continue to get legally married once they start a family. But marriage has become less of a necessity for society to accept a relationship between two people for younger, childbearing folk.

Given the fact that we, seniors, as a group, are no longer interested in procreating, it has become even less of a necessity.

RELATIONSHIPS IN THE SENIOR WORLD TODAY

There was a time when a sexual relationship between older folks appeared "unseemly," "inappropriate," "ugly," "laughable," and according to some religious tenets, "unholy," even "demonic."

The very good news is that our society has gotten over its phobias against relationships between older folks. As you have read, not only does our society now accept relationships among older folks, but society has come to see there is plenty of money to be earned when seniors seek to engage in dating and mating each other: Anti-aging products are big sellers. So are sexual enhancements. Travel companies gear trips specifically to the less energetic senior. Case in point: dating sites just for seniors have become a billion-dollar business.

We can now move from my conversations with seniors about their views on dating, mating, and their mortality to what they feel like being in a relationship as they approach their twilight years.

A relationship between two seniors is much harder to define because, by and large, we do not have the label "married" to guide us. When we make the move from a dating relationship to a bonding relationship, how do we know we have bonded? When our relationship moves from dating to mating, do we need to make a commitment, verbally, legally—or can it just happen?

What makes a relationship a relationship? How does it differ from dating?

Originally when I started out, I used as a baseline that two people are in a relationship if they see each other naked or are naked together at some point. And they see each other, be with each other, more than 50% of the time.

I found that both of these baselines were artificial, and therefore, incorrect.

I noted that in a nursing/rehab/assisted living facility there are folks who describe themselves in a relationship despite never being undressed together. And I've come across folks who tell me they have a relationship with someone even though they have sporadic contacts with their special ones. In both scenarios, the folks described a chemistry between them bonding each to each other. They described the chemistry as including a loyalty to each other, a feeling of guilt toward the other, and basic caring for the other.

So my baseline has become, simply, if someone tells me he or she is in a relationship, then he or she is! All they need to say is that the relationship feels different than the relationship they have with their children, their siblings, their friends, etc. The chemistry is different.

I realize it's going to be impossible to describe all the different chemical bonding relationships between two people. There are so many nuances.

WHY PARTNER AT ALL

We do not have to go back to Adam and Eve to understand that humans were meant to partner. We did not have to read Freud's theories in Chapter 3, "Sex and the Single Senior." We do not need to see a psychiatrist, a psychologist, or a spiritualist to learn the need to partner. We just need to partner. Look around you. Read the newspapers, visit other societies. So much is designated by twos.

So I rely on true stories to tell the story.

Before I begin, I will stress once again, the only description of a relationship between two people I can offer is that they, either together or separately, tell me they are in a relationship.

When we make the move from a dating relationship to a bonding relationship, how do we know we have bonded? When our relationship moves from dating to mating, do we need to make a commitment, verbally, legally—or can it just happen?

Therefore, the one question I asked of every senior I met, including those who did not want to be interviewed to any great extent, was, "Are you in a relationship? And if not, why aren't you in a relationship?"

Most of this chapter is going to be descriptions of different seniors who are in relationships. You will see the "fifty shades"—the variety among seniors—of relationships.

But the world of single seniors does contain a number of folk who prefer to be alone. That fact is not much different from younger folk. Among younger folk, you will also find a percentage of people who have no interest in having a special person in their lives. So, we start our conversation about relationships by talking about those seniors who have elected not to be in a relationship.

NO RELATIONSHIP BECAUSE
I LOVE MY FREEDOM

Those seniors who say they eschew relationships because they love their freedom assume a relationship requires either living together all the time, or at least most of the time. They cite a litany of traits and habits and interests they've accumulated over the years that they would have to give up if they are in a relationship. They want to dress the way they do, want to walk around na ked in their house, blare music all day long, watch the TV shows they want to watch. They admit they "hardly sleep at night," "snore like blazes," "must turn on the light during the night and read, write, watch television," "cook some eggs," "drink a glass of water," and (lordy, lordy), "go to the bathroom like it seems all the time." The men watch "porn" or "travel" or "military" or an "action-oriented" movie. For women it might be an infomercial selling beauty creams or pots and pans, jewelry, diet drugs—whatever.

Senior women expressed physical embarrassment. I heard "scars from surgery," "bad breath from post-menopausal hormonal change," "need to cream and lotion myself to death," and other self-conscious comments.

From senior men, I heard the need to maintain an image of being strong. "Open a jar;" "change a light bulb;" "carry the suitcase." They did not want to be seen as weak or tired.

NO RELATIONSHIP BECAUSE
I CANNOT FIND ANYONE

Those folks who say "I've looked and looked but there is no one out there" have developed a cynicism in order to protect themselves from getting hurt. They lump the opposite gender into a monolithic group.

From women, I've heard men are looking only for a "nurse or a purse" more times than I care to repeat. Men are too needy. They want a cook, a cleaner, a housekeeper. All they want is sex. They all want a younger woman. The only thing stopping a guy from chasing a younger woman is that a younger woman is too expensive.

From men, I hear women are too much of a burden. They want this or that. They want "to change me." They want to dress me differently, change my habits. They want to be taken care of financially. They demand I be romantic. They constantly want to be "deserved." They just put too much pressure on me to be something I may not be.

— Elizabeth —

Elizabeth is eighty-five. She was widowed at seventy-five. Elizabeth says, "I am too old and too busy to have another relationship." She is in relatively good health, has children, grandchildren, and yes, even two great-grandchildren. It's a close family. There is no contact on a daily basis, but they keep her in the family loop, "keeping me feeling loved." She has plenty of friends because she belongs to a few clubs and attends church functions. She has subscriptions to events and travels every few months to visit family and/or friends.

She admits she still misses her marriage. No, it wasn't only that her husband was such a great guy, but she misses those special moments, the camaraderie, the in-sync quality she believes only marriage can bring.

And then, she adds, she lacks the energy. "I am feeling too old to do the work, to meet and maintain a relationship with a new someone."

As our conversation progressed, Elizabeth became less introspective, more open, and less guarded. Eventually, our conversation ended with Elizabeth flashing a bright smile, saying, "I can't wait to read your book. Maybe it will get me going again."

— Frank —

Frank has been hanging around a club bar off and on for the past fifteen years, ever since his divorce. He is now in his early eighties, and has just broken off with his younger girlfriend, Leyla, a woman in her late fifties. They had been going together for five years. She lives in the Bronx. He lives in Manhattan. He would stay at her home on one weekend. She would come into Manhattan the next weekend to stay with him. So what broke them up? "She was getting too involved with my family issues. I told her to back off, but she couldn't." He explained he was having problems with his thirty-five-year-old daughter, and his girlfriend put her "two cents" in. His girlfriend was very critical of his daughter's behavior. "I couldn't tolerate that. She is my daughter. Leyla overstepped the boundaries of our relationship." Then Frank went on to generalize, "All women, sooner or later, will run your life if you let them. That's why I've never allowed my relationships to go any further than weekend romances." Frank insisted that he will never get involved again. He admitted he is lonely once again. And that's why he is hanging around once again his favorite bar and drinking too much.

FIFTY SHADES OF RELATIONSHIPS

As we will see in the following stories, many seniors have found many ways to navigate around their negative feelings and express happiness they have someone of their own.

Let us start with the obvious. MARRIAGE. Marriage has been *traditionally* defined as a legal agreement between one man and one woman by which they promise to live together in the relationship of husband and wife. Marriage changes the relationship between the parties, giving husband and wife new rights and obligations. Traditionally, government agencies have used this legal agreement to award benefits, such as IRS tax deductions for married couples. Marriage is a legal relationship controlled by government rules and regulations. Marriage is done by the "book," including a blood test and a trip to City Hall for the license if the state requires. A legal marriage, whether or not the woman changes her name.

We all know that marriage has undergone tremendous changes in our generation. We use the expression, *non-traditional marriage*. Many of us in our seventies, eighties, and nineties are in non-traditional marriages—meaning we live together acting like a husband and wife, but are not legally bound.

Yet seniors talk about marriage wistfully or defensively, as it if is the platonic ideal of a relationship. So why are they not *marrying* in their seventies, eighties, nineties? Most of it has to do with all that has been written in the earlier chapters.

When the word is mentioned, seniors admit at their age it is difficult for them to feel comfortable in a 24/7 relationship. A 24/7 relationship leaves them too exposed. Sleeping together in the same bed, seeing each other naked constantly, is a much tougher road at eighty then it was at fifty.

They either sleep in separate beds in the same bedroom, or, as I found where the couples are wealthier, they keep totally separate bedrooms. Even a king-sized bed has become too disturbing for the other partner.

When talking to my still-married, partnered friends in their sixties to nineties, they tell me they continue to maintain the same sleeping arrangements they had when they were first married. But now, in their later years, they are waking up during the night and walking around. One partner or the other often ends up on a couch, in a guest room, not wanting to disturb their mate or be disturbed by their bed partner any further.

However, the first time this becomes a "decision-making option" is when we are changing or relating to new partners in our sixties to nineties. For those seniors who are now living together 24/7, almost all of them told me they do not sleep together.

The fact is, the older you get, the worse you sleep. "The Older You Are, the Worse You Sleep" is actually the title of a column written by Matthew Walker in the *Wall Street Journal*, dated Oct. 14, 2017. In it, he states that your ability to sleep through the night begins to deteriorate earlier than you might think. "Passing into your mid-to late forties, age will have stripped you of 60% to 70% of the deep sleep you were enjoying as a teen. By the time you reach age seventy, you will have lost 80% to 90% of your youthful, restorative deep sleep."

When we live with someone, it's hard to hide and keep ourselves alluring. We can overcome these negatives by maintaining separate bedrooms. Keep separate bedrooms.

Keeping separate bedrooms is a little simpler and sexier than trying to get over our phobias or change our habits. So put your money into buying more physical space, not into marriage counseling. Invest in a two-bedroom house or apartment.

The beauty of this is when family or friends come to stay with you, you move in together, into one bedroom. When they leave, you claim back your privacy.

If living together is a must-have, take the advice from other seniors and opt for separate but equal bedrooms.

Once the matter of marriage was off the table, out of the conversation, I found that men were less forthcoming about admitting they were in a relationship. Or even describing a relationship. Men say they really don't waste time or energy trying to describe their relationship with a woman, other than things like "It's been a while...how long I don't remember, but it's been a while that we've been together." When I ask what the relationship is like, many shrug their shoulders. The one thing they verbalize is that she does not sleep with anyone else. If she does, that's a dealbreaker. I asked them if they ever bring up, spontaneously, that they are engaged in a relationship when they are with a group of guys watching a game at a bar, fishing, or playing poker. Most men responded, "No." They said they might talk about the attractiveness of women in general, or comment about the women generally if they are in a public place. Those who said "yes" stated they like to show off their woman and will generally pull her picture out of their wallet. No further description of the relationship. Men rarely, if ever, talk about their particular relationship with a particular woman.

— Joanne —

For those of us who have had one partner all those years, more or less into our sixties, we do not pay attention to the changes in our sleep habits. Except for Joanne, I interviewed no one who had a separate bedroom from day one of their marriage.

Joanne expressed surprise at this line of my questions to her. She is an American. But she was totally enamored with Italy. Actually, everything Italian. It probably had to do with the fact that her dad was a teacher of Italian in one of the universities in New York.

After her graduation from an Ivy League college in the 1950s, she took off for Italy, not to return for fifty years. She married twice and was widowed twice. As an interesting aside, Joanne married a Duke and a Marquis. Joanne returned to New York, a widow in her late seventies, alone, no children, but with two titles: a Duchess and a Marquesa. In both marriages Joanne and her titled husbands maintained separate bedrooms. "In Europe, it is the norm." Joanne probably meant for those folks we would call the upper class. So how did it affect your sexual relations, I asked. She stated that while she had no ability to compare her sexual activity as a married woman occupying her own space with others who did not, she pointed out that her husbands never complained. And she didn't either. She added, looking me straight in the eye, that her sex was good. "My men loved me, and I loved them. We had our differences and arguments in our marriage, as I am sure you did in your marriage, but my sex life was just as good if not better than anybody else's."

Today, Joanne is almost eighty. She has had a boyfriend for the past five years, meeting him at one of her college's club meet-ups. Joanne, in my opinion, is a success story. She missed having someone in her life. She put her fears, nerves, and judgments aside, and put herself out there again to meet a man. She once again has a man in her life—after Medicare.

MY STORY – *Continued*

I can speak from personal experience. I was supposed to get remarried about two years after I became a widow. Marriage was very important to me. A legal marriage. After all, I had been married for forty-four years. It was the only kind of formal sexual bonding relationship that I knew. Somewhere in the back of my mind, I believed that "marriage would make an honest woman out of me." As you recall my story from the chapters "Money, Money, Money," and "Kids Are The New In-Laws," a legal marriage later in life can be financially costly and frowned upon by the children of the parties involved. So we decided not to marry legally, but instead, just have a religious marriage. We were amazed to learn that my pastor was happy to preside over an Episcopal marriage, in church, with all the trimmings, even though we did not have that legal document. We called it a commitment ceremony. There are even wedding rings that are for sale, but called "commitment" rings. Then we were supposed to move in together. Edward was to move into my apartment, as I was the one with the two bedrooms. But then he refused. He wanted to keep it as it was. Live apart, but still be "committed to each other."

At the time, I was devastated. I told him that I didn't want to be his perennial girlfriend, his perennial date, his perennial "arm-candy." I gave him back his engagement ring, and threw him out of my house. Yes, I did. Just like the movies. For me, it was marriage and living together or *nothing.*

I felt demeaned by Edward. I knew that I needed to get over my devastation by re-entering the senior social world. So, for the first time, I went on a singles dating site. I was so hurt and angry at the time that I wrote in my dating profile, "Please, please do not even approach me if you honestly do not want to live with a woman, or are in fear of outliving your money. I've had my heart broken already, since my widowhood of two years ago."

I met my current boyfriend online. We have been dating for over four years. We see each other most weekends. He lives in a home in Westchester. I live in Manhattan. When I visit him, I enter his world. I've helped him hang pictures, garden, go to his supermarket. When he comes down to my apartment, he helps me fix things around the house. We take trips together. We also take trips alone. He still skis. He goes fishing with his friends. I've traveled to visit girlfriends in D.C., went to a country western concert in Oklahoma, and visited my family without him. Our relationship is easy and obliging. Our separation is non-threatening to each other. We assume the other is not cheating on the other. I do not think either of us have any sense of jealousy or possessiveness about each other. Those seem to be emotions that are much stronger with younger folk.

We have different last names, obviously. Most folks who meet us simply assume we are married. We look married, whatever that means. However, folks, being politically polite or correct, often seem awkward as they address us. Folks seem to be more comfortable with us as a couple when they understand the relationship more fully.

At first, or at an early meeting, I always take the lead. To you ladies who are reading this book, please take this piece of advice. It is up to you to state the "state of the relationship." Men, as a group, simply look the other way, shift their feet...and don't know what to say.

I like to say, in mixed company, "No, we are not married. I am a merry widow. And Jack is sowing his wild oats." That gets a laugh. One awkward moment in a social situation out of the way. Other times, when I am feeling particularly naughty, and Jack is not around, I might say, "I am a merry widow, and Jack is my boy toy." I usually say that to the woman when we are alone. This comment is just woman's locker room talk. Yes, we can brag as much as men do when they are alone. Trust me on this one. The first chance she gets, she will repeat that to her guy.

Jack, for his part, at seventy-five years old, gray-haired, lined face, bad back, just loves hearing he is sowing his wild oats. He straightens up a bit and smiles with a look of virility shining out from his eyes. To you women, try this out. No matter what your relationship is...short of a formal engagement: "I am a merry divorcee (or widow) and _____ is sowing his wild oats."

Is there any jealousy or possessiveness even though we spend more time without each other than with each other? Not a scintilla. Jack's ex-wife is with him for a few hours almost every day for ostensibly business reasons. When Christmas comes, he has his tree up with his kids, grandkids, and ex-wife sharing presents. I go to Boston to visit my two sons and grandkids, sharing Christmas presents. We have what I call a well-balanced relationship. I feel that Jack is into me sexually, as I am into him. In other words, I am confident that the sexual energy between us, whether or not we are together, cements our relationship.

What will happen in the future, I have no idea. We never talk about marriage, or commitment. For me, I am just going with the flow. I am definitely bonded to him. I care deeply for him. And for me, our sex is the best! I ask for little else.

Looking back to my relationship with Edward, I see I have changed from my need to be married. Perhaps life's experience has changed me. I no longer believe that marriage is the only way to prove to myself that I have a worthwhile, happy, and long-term relationship. I am religious, but I now see God as more flexible and willing to accept my altered state of relationship. I see the practicality, the desirability, and yes, even the beauty of not tying the knot in my senior years.

— Stephen —

I interviewed Steve by telephone. I met his niece socially at a party. When I told her that I am writing this book, she looked at me with a grin on her face, and said, "You MUST call my uncle. He lives in Chicago and will be very forthcoming." So I dutifully called Steve.

Steve at the time was eighty-five. He said he was a very healthy eighty-five-year-old and goes regularly to a large gym on the south side of Chicago. He met "the love of his life" at eighty. He went online for "months and months" until this one clicked. He confessed to her that he lied in his profile and took ten years off his age. Then she confessed. She wrote she was seventy, but she, too, was eighty. After a while, they saw that they were a couple. Living separately at opposite ends of town became too much of a burden for the relationship. Neither of them had children, so decision-making was not complicated. They could not decide who should move in with whom, so at the late age of eighty-three, they each sold their respective homes and moved into an apartment together. As he said, "I could follow my heart." As of this writing, they are not married. Unnecessary and expensive, says Steve. Jokingly, he says, "She doesn't need the pressure of trying to remember a new name at this stage of her life."

— Marvin —

Marvin is another eighty-five-year-old. He's been single, as he says, with a smile, "forever." By forever, he meant that since the death of his second wife when he was seventy-nine, he has been in and out of relationships, like a "rabbit." "Why?" I ask. Because I finally learned how to have a happy childhood. Marvin's childhood (I think he was referring more to his adolescence), and it seems indeed, both of his marriages, were staid and conservative. Finally, at the ripe age of seventy-nine years old, thrust into the singles' world once again, Marvin has learned not to take himself, and the relationship seriously. Marvin said, "Now I am out for fun." A sense of mortality is liberating, he states. "I learned to text. And I text dirty. I love texting dirty." He smiles. And she loves texting back. We both laugh a lot and call each other sexy. I am not interested in what you girls call finding a "soulmate." I want company, and good company. I want someone who makes me laugh and makes me feel good about myself.

You might think that Marvin is having a great time in bed. Well, think again. Marvin no longer can "get it up." No longer can he "get it in." He stopped taking Viagra a long time ago. But he can cuddle...and loves it. He loves to touch his girlfriend, and they try things that he would have called illicit when he was younger. They "play" with each other in the movies, in front of the television, whatever. "The only thing that keeps me back from displaying my newfound sexual freedom in public is that I don't want to get arrested." He laughs a bit when he says this. I think Marvin has learned to combine his fantasies with his reality. But, no matter, it is clear to me that Marvin is the living proof of, "It's never too late to have a happy childhood." He has three children, and seven grandchildren, with whom he maintains close contact. All his girlfriends have also had large, close-knit families. So, Marvin says, his relationships with his women have been very balanced.

— Margaret —

Margaret lives alone in a two-bedroom apartment on Fifth Avenue. She comes from a monied family, so she went to private schools, traveled greatly, and lived what you and I might call a "storied" childhood. She worked for a few years as an actress, and proudly stated that she did go to acting school. She never married. She keeps herself very attractive today, at seventy-nine. But she was quick to say that she had all sorts of physical problems as an adolescent, which she feels prevented her from the typical social scene of adolescent awakening to her own sexuality. When she finally began to date in a serious way, she was well into her thirties, and felt out of joint. She stated candidly that she never enjoyed sex. Hated parting her legs, felt pain, not pleasure in her vagina when her guy "finger-fucked" her.

Well, I asked, "Margaret, are you lonely?" Her answer was surprising. She said "No." In her forties, she met a man who simply "wowed" her. But he lived on the west coast. She had become too entrenched in her east coast life to want to move to the west coast. Then, she adds, she fell in love with someone so far away because it protected her from the pain of physical intimacy on a 24/7 basis. She told me that she is not lonely, but she feels they are a couple, are bonded, and have been for more than thirty years. They get together three to four times a year, either on the east coast or the west coast. They are affectionate with each other. They hold hands, hug. They laugh at each other's jokes and foibles. They talk on the phone often. They did Skype a bit...but lost interest in actually looking at each other when they spoke. They have gone on trips together, on cruises, mostly. But Margaret entertains with lovely, sumptuous parties, alone. Margaret travels to visit friends and family alone. Most certainly, Margaret lives alone.

Margaret denied feeling lonely. This relationship is enough for her to make her feel complete. And how she feels about it is the only thing that counts. Hearing his voice is a high. Traveling together is great. It's enough for her!

— Sonia —

Sonia is a wealthy widow. She continues to live in her three-bedroom Park Avenue apartment, despite the fact that her children have long since moved out into their own lives and apartments, and she has been totally alone. I met her by chance at a club that my husband and I belonged to in New York. She started talking to us at one of those cocktail events. Within the first five minutes of meeting, she informed us that she had become a widow, and purposely joined this club to meet a man. Did we know any men we could introduce to her? I was a bit put off by her forwardness. But then I simply said to myself...this is a woman who knows what she wants.

I later heard through the grapevine that she met a man at a legal event held in Florida. Her late husband was a lawyer and belonged to a number of organizations. She was aware of these organizations, and she simply continued to go to these events alone, as a widow.

She came down with multiple sclerosis. She kept dating anyway. Today, her multiple sclerosis keeps her confined to a wheelchair. But anyway, her partner (as she refers to him), continues to come in from New Jersey on the weekends. They spend a quiet Friday evening in her spacious apartment, watching television, catching up on each other's family and friends. On Saturday, depending on the weather, he either wheels her or taxis with her to some New York attraction. They love going to a movie. They enjoy dinner in a local restaurant. Sunday, he returns to New Jersey. "Anything physical?" I ask Sonia. She smiles. "I feel his warmth in his smile. I know he loves me. I love to kiss his penis. He loves me to touch him. We are as intimate as we can be. We are as excited to be with each other as 'two teenagers.' Bed is the great equalizer. We both have as much energy as we need."

So many relationships are acknowledged in ways today not thought of ten years ago.

There is something called a "Commitment Ceremony." "Friendship (or Friendship with Benefits) Ceremony." Friendship rings. Commitment rings. Google these words for yourself...and see what comes up. Businesses are on Google to service any of these in-between, off-the-grid relationships.

— **Ruth** —

It's impossible for me to describe my relationship to Paul. We live apart. We have our own lives. I visit my children and grandchildren without him. He visits his family without me. Each of our families barely knows that we have a significant other. But to each other, we are significant. I just know it. He's there when I want him. He's there when I need him. He has never let me down. I really don't ask that much of him. It's hard for him to get around. It's also hard for me to get around. We never spent Christmas together. We never spent Thanksgiving together. Or Easter for that matter. Come to think of it, we never spend any of the big holidays together. But it's not important for our relationship. Our relationship is balanced, between us and our families. We both agree. So there are no problems involved. We get together, usually once or twice a week. We visit each other. Or we go out. Or we go to a movie. Or we double date. Whatever. It's just nice to know there is someone out there. He's happy to see me. I just know that.

We are very affectionate to each other. But we no longer sleep at each other's houses. Neither of us want to spend the night. It's just too much work.

— David —

I've been in a relationship with Shirley about twelve years now. She was my third girlfriend after my divorce from my wife of thirty-five years. I got divorced at sixty-three. I met Shirley when I was around seventy-two. She sort of grew on me. No, it was not love at first sight. At our age, who are you kidding when you say you fell in love? She was in my class at the Y. It just sort of grew, week after week. Maybe that's why it's lasting so long. It became physical slowly...after a bunch of months went by. We weren't that compatible at first, but our sexual relationship also grew, little by little. We talked it out a number of times. Now she's become special for me. We are talking about giving up homes, either selling them or renting them out. She doesn't want to move into my home. I don't want to move into her home. So we would need to find a third home. Which brings me to the idea of a retirement community. Lots of my friends have moved to a retirement community. I am sort of jealous of them. They are long-term marriages...so they were able to make the move fairly easily. I'm different, because my divorce threw me a curve. But I'm back on track, and we are beginning to plan our future together.

I love the idea of having a future again.

There are probably more than Fifty Shades of Relationships out there in our senior years. What's important is that it works for you both. If you smile to yourself when you think of him or her. If you feel his/her presence in your life. If, like Margaret, despite the fact that to an outsider you may look totally alone, you are proud and happy you are enjoying your God-given right to have a relationship your way, until the day you die—then go for it.

Remember, these are your Golden Years. Remember, this is Our Time. Make the most of it.

***

CONCLUSION

THIS BOOK IS NOT ABOUT HOW TO DATE, OR WHAT to do on a date. It is not about how to establish a relationship. It is not a guidebook. It is not specifically a self-help book. It is a Report of many conversations between seniors of what is actually going on in the world of senior singles. It is a Report added with my research and comments.

This book actually has no conclusion. Dating and Mating stories can go on and on.

I heard lots on relationships that went sour, dates that were good, and others that were not. I heard lots about seniors' success with one way of meeting new people. Then I heard the opposite.

I generalized on the dating and mating habits and attitudes of seniors only when enough of my interviewees seemed to agree on a point.

As we lawyers say, "Where there is a preponderance of evidence." What I've decided to do, here, is simply quote comments from my interviewees on their dating and mating experiences. You will recognize some of these quotes from the text. The others are in my notes, but I didn't use them.

Here are some additional comments from the many seniors with whom I met or talked to. They are contradictory, at times. But life itself is full of contradictions. Hopefully, you will get some ideas, or identify with some of these comments and take them to heart:

"Always keep a smile on your face. A smile is very sexy."

"Listen and ask questions. Don't talk too much."

"Show high spirits. Strong personality is sexy."

"Never try to sleep or have sex with a first date."

"Have sex by the fifth date. You need to get it out of the way. It's easier to have sex than to feel emotionally connected. Feeling emotionally connected takes more time."

"Older folks should have sex much later, well after we have bonded on other levels." "When you are older, a relationship takes longer to develop. Be patient. You are set in your ways, and not sure where you can negotiate, or duck when necessary."

"When you are older, a relationship is easier to develop. You know yourself better. You have the confidence and experience. Don't deny it."

"Life begins when we want it to begin."

"Stay away from Internet dating sites. Everyone lies. Too many folks are dangerous."

"Internet dating is the best way to meet someone new. Takes less energy, less expensive, better able to rule a potential in or out."

"First impressions are hugely important. Never forget that."

"First impressions are meaningless. Take the time to learn more."

"Your kids will keep you from making any mistake."

"Watch out for your kids. They really couldn't care less what's best for you."

"For every pot, there is a cover. There is someone out there for you."

"The senior world is loaded with broken hearts and broken people. Forget the whole thing."

"Who would want an old bag like me?"

"I'd rather be with someone in my own age group than have the pressure of someone too young for me."

"You're never too old to have a happy childhood."

"I am too old to fall in love."

"I fall in love more easily now than I did when I was younger. Let me correct that. I become more infatuated more easily now than when I was younger."

"I still get turned on."

"I can't get turned on anymore. It comes slow."

"My lights are on, but my voltage is low."

"I always keep my sense of humor about my sex life."

"I've outgrown virgins. I like veterans."

"Looks make no difference to me now. In the dark, all cats are gray."

"I told my girlfriend that I really enjoyed myself, but I wish she were better looking."

"I hated his big nose. She said, 'What do you care? You are not going to have his children.' That was the moment I started relaxing about the whole thing."

"I'm more attracted to widows. They seem more virginal."

"I like older women. They have more money. Are more independent. Easier to be with."

"I try to go out with women at least twenty years younger than I am. I am strong and virile, and I have enough money to afford it. I want to be seen with a trophy woman at my club. I want other men to eat their hearts out."

"I stopped trying to date. Can't handle the anxiety."

"I use a tranquillizer before I meet a woman for the first time. My nerves aren't what they used to be."

"My guy needs up to an hour before he ejaculates. I feel beautiful and needed by servicing him in this way. We have the time. Thank god I still have the energy. When he comes, I am happier."

"I've stopped looking. There's nobody out there. Men are all scum. They only want to get sex. They do not want to give anything. For example, that starts with picking up a check! Be sure you put that in your book."

"I am fine with paying my own way. I expect the man to pay his own way. That puts us on an equal footing. But I still want him to open a car door for me, hold an umbrella for us, take my arm when we cross the street. You know what I mean—plain, old-fashioned good manners."

"Nothing gives me greater pleasure than walking down the street holding my guy's hand."

"I come more easily now than I did when I was younger. Don't know why, but I do."

"A relationship needs work—at any age. And that includes myself in as good condition as I can—both physically and emotionally. I keep a positive attitude to life. Say my aphorisms to myself every morning. I wish all singles in their later years would pay attention to what I am saying."

"I'm not what I used to be. But what the hell, just keep trying. If there is a woman out there who wants a really sweet, kind lover, here I am. If Rockefeller could do it, so can I."

"Beauty is in the eyes of the beholder."

"Beauty is not in the eyes of the beholder. It's in the eyes of the woman. Nothing sexier than eyes."

"Attractiveness is in the eyes of the beholder."

"Attractiveness is a sexual energy coming at me from the person I am talking to."

"Sexual attraction, attractiveness, desire, wish to be with someone—no matter what you call it—is something that we have, like it or not."

"All men want is either a nurse or a purse."

"I'm a merry widow. I am having fun. What more is there to say?"

"I love calling my seventy-six-year-old boyfriend, my 'boy-toy.'"

"Living together is a killer at any age. It's even worse after sixty-five."

"I've given up looking for my soulmate."

"It's never too late to find your soulmate. I think I found him here, in my assisted living home."

"It's easier finding someone today than it was when I was in my sixties."

"Love is not a constant. It wasn't when we were younger. Why should we expect it to be now?"

"My kids are watching over me, especially now when I am letting my needs overcome the practical side of life."

"My kids have become my biggest pain in the ass."

"Stop being so practical in your last trimester of your life. You can't take it with you."

"I've haven't changed a bit since my twenties."

"Every age is a growing and changing experience."

"I have the perfect girlfriend. She leaves me alone."

"I have the perfect boyfriend. He leaves me alone."

"Enough of this interview. Can you introduce me to any of your subjects?"

***

AFTERWORD

AS WE FACE THE LAST TRIMESTER OF OUR LIVES, remember, it is not over until it's over. We need not be lonely now. This book has been an invitation to experience life to the fullest...to acknowledge our sexuality even as we age; to live with it; to include it going forward in our last trimester.

I have attempted to explain the landscape to you. Continue to experience life, and enjoy the ride down the river to the mouth of the great beyond. If you are already in the boat...do not jump ship until the day you die.

So please keep that in mind when you think of how you want to live these next twenty years, give or take a few.

Visit me and the rest of us at my websites:

- **ResetMyClock.com**
- **SecretsofDatingandMatingAfterMedicare.com**
- **HappydaysAfter60.com**

Let us all take this journey together.

Made in the USA
Las Vegas, NV
04 December 2022

61138417R00115